Sure Signs of Heavenly Hope

... And 30 Other Bible-Based Meditations

Series # 7

Roger Ellsworth

Unless otherwise noted, Scripture quotations are taken from the New King James Version®. Copyright © 1982 by Thomas Nelson. Used by permission. All rights reserved.

Copyright © 2018, Roger Ellsworth

All rights reserved. No part of this book may be reproduced, scanned, or distributed in any printed or electronic form without permission.

First Edition: 2018

ISBN: 978-0-9988812-1-8

20180829LSI

Great Writing Publications
www.greatwriting.org
Taylors, SC

www.greatwriting.org

Purpose

My Coffee Cup Meditations are short, easy-to-read, engagingly presented devotions based on the Bible, the Word of God. Each reading takes a single idea or theme and develops it in a thought-provoking way so that you are inspired to consider the greatness of God, the relevance of the good news of the life, death, resurrection, and coming-again of Jesus, and are better equipped for life in this world and well prepared for the world to come.

www.mycoffeecupmeditations.com

https://www.facebook.com/MyCoffeeCupMeditations/

Dedication

To my Pastor and his wife:

Justin and Anna Wainscott

About This Book

This book is the result of the labors Roger Ellsworth and the thought he has given to various passages of Scripture over the years. You may read more about Roger on page 141.

We hope you will enjoy these Bible-based meditations. We would love to hear from you, so please send us a note to tell us what you think—which ones you liked most, and how they made a difference in your life or in the life of a family member, friend, or work associate. To reach us online, go to www.mycoffeecupmeditations.com/contact

MY COFFEE-CUP MEDITATIONS

Table of Contents

1 Sure Signs of Heavenly Hope 16
2 A Doctor Thanks a Sick Man 20
3 The Tent of Meeting 24
4 "But God" (1) 28
5 "But God" (2) 32
6 A Deed to Win Your Heart! 36
7 Gone to the Birds 40
8 A Good Meeting 44
9 Bright Truths for Bleak Times 48
10 Today Thy Mercy Calls Us 52
11 Drops and Showers 56
12 A Great Man 60
13 A Young Girl 64
14 Mr. False Assumptions 68
15 Clean! 72
16 Where is My Heart? 76
17 Buying Bread 80
18 Come and Go 84
19 Prayer: Important and Difficult 88
20 Things That Help Me Pray: Loading up on the Privilege 92
21 Things That Help Me Pray: Loading up on the Purchase 96
22 Things That Help Me Pray: Loading Up on Praise 100
23 Things That Help Me Pray: Lightening the Load 104
24 Keep on Praying! 108
25 "Help, I Have Done Awful Things!" 112

26 "Help, I'm Disappointed with God!" 116
27 "Help, I Find It Hard to Believe!" 120
28 "Help, I Think God Isn't Fair!" 124
29 "Help, I Think God Has Forgotten Me!" 128
30 Purchasing and Preserving 132
31 Wisdom from Annie Johnson Flint 136

About the Author 141
The Series 142

The App

www.mycoffeecupmeditations.com

Be sure you get the app!

-1-

From God's Word, the Bible...

And if Christ is not risen, your faith is futile; you are still in your sins! Then also those who have fallen asleep in Christ have perished. If in this life only we have hope in Christ, we are of all men the most pitiable.

1 Corinthians 15:17-19

Sure Signs of Heavenly Hope

The time had come for my eighth and final sermon in a conference for Brazilian pastors and their wives. Organized and promoted by Missionary Richard Denham, it was a well-attended conference with approximately 800 registrants.

The Scripture I chose for this final sermon was 1 Thessalonians 4:13-18, the passage in which the Apostle Paul gloriously wipes away the concerns of his readers about their loved ones who had died in faith in the Lord Jesus Christ.

I divided the sermon into three parts—two kinds of sorrows, four blessed events, and one crucial condition. The two kinds of sorrows Paul indicates in verse 13 are sorrowing with hope and sorrowing without hope. The four blessed events he lays out in verses 14-17 are the return of the Lord, the resurrection of dead believers, the rapture of living believers, and the meeting in the air. The one crucial condition is stated by Paul in these words: "… if we believe that Jesus died and rose again ..." (v. 14). The glorious future Paul lays out in this passage is only for those who trust in the redeeming work of the Lord Jesus Christ.

As I brought the sermon to a close, it occurred to me that it was very doubtful that I would ever see any of my hearers again in this life. So I closed with these words: "It's very likely that I will never see you again in this life, but I *will* see you again." As I made that closing statement I pointed upward with my index finger, indicating that marvelous meeting in the air.

After we sang our closing song and prayed our closing prayer, these wonderful people began coming to me one after the other to bid farewell. I couldn't speak their language—Portuguese—and they couldn't speak mine, and my interpreter was nowhere to be seen. But I soon discovered that we didn't need him as we had a common language after all. It was the language of smiles, tears, and uplifted index fingers. Yes, as they said their goodbyes to me, these Brazilian brothers and sisters in Christ would point upward. That was each one's way of saying: "I will meet you in the air."

I remember very well the loud, boisterous singing of those precious people. I recall how their love for the preaching of God's Word seemed to make them hang on every word. I haven't forgotten their warmth and friendliness. But the memory I treasure most is those uplifted fingers. Those fingers were signs of the common hope that Christians share.

How much the Scriptures make of that hope! It is our "blessed" hope (Titus 2:13). It is "sure and steadfast" (Heb. 6:19). It is our "living" hope (1 Peter 1:3). It is the hope of "eternal life" that has been promised to all believers by the God "who cannot lie" (Titus 1:2).

The hope of Christians puts a wide, yawning chasm between them and unbelievers. When unbelievers speak of hope, they are probably referring to a desire or yearning for something that may or may not come true. They hope that life will bring them health, happiness, and material success, and that they will be free from difficulties and calamities. And, of course, they hope for the same for their children and grandchildren. But such things are by no means certain. Christians most certainly share this kind of hope and the uncertainty that comes along with it. But that kind of hope is limited to this life. The great hope of Christians lies beyond this life, and it is a sure and certain hope. It is the hope of that meeting in the air and of eternal life in heaven.

Unbelievers consider that great hope to be as unsure as all other hopes. They think Christians believe it merely because they want it to be true, and that there is no foundation for it. A twentieth-century American philosopher once said of faith that it may be defined briefly as "an illogical belief in the occurrence of the improbable."[1]

Christians laugh at that definition and look to the resurrection of Jesus as the foundation for their hope. If Jesus arose, we shall arise, and if He lives, we shall live (John 14:19). On that basis, I will lift my finger and point upward.

---

[1] H.L. Mencken, https://www.goodreads.com/quotes/4690-faith-may-be-defined-briefly-as-an-illogical-belief-in

-2-

From God's Word, the Bible...

But we are bound to give thanks to God always for you, brethren beloved by the Lord, because God from the beginning chose you for salvation through sanctification by the Spirit and belief in the truth, to which He called you by our gospel, for the obtaining of the glory of our Lord Jesus Christ.

2 Thessalonians 2:13-14

A Doctor Thanks a Sick Man

When I went to the conference mentioned in the previous reading, I had some concern about eating. Some of my friends, who were quite experienced in the area of foreign travel, told me that it could be very difficult to suddenly transition to eating a different kind of food. So when I arrived at the conference center, I began to ask the few English-speaking people I could find about what I should and should not eat. One told me to refrain from eating the meat. Another told me that I should not eat the vegetables. Yet another told me to stay away from the fruit. It occurred to me that I was quickly running out of things to eat! I decided that the best strategy was to eat a little bit of the same food each day. So I did, and I got sick—very sick! I began to wonder if I would be able to fulfill each of my preaching assignments.

When I conveyed my situation to Richard Denham, the missionary who engaged me to come to Brazil, he told me that he knew a doctor who was attending the conference and would ask her to see me. A more gracious lady one could never expect to meet. When I thanked her for making time for me, I was much surprised by her response. With tears welling up, she said: "You don't need to thank me. I need to thank you for coming to preach the Word of God to us."

Preaching is to be done with the eye trained on God's approval and not on the listener's. But if a hearer is blessed by the preaching, there certainly isn't anything wrong with him or her conveying that to the preacher. Preachers need that kind of encouragement, and most of us would say that we have often been blessed to receive it. In the area of favorable responses I have received, this doctor's was in a class by itself. It was more heartfelt and genuine than any other. It wasn't because of any spectacular ability that I possess as a preacher; it was rather due to what I was preaching—the Word of God.

This doctor made a connection that appears to be increasingly rare. She understood that if we value God's Word, we must also value the preaching that declares it.

Preaching has fallen into disfavor. Some pastor search committees reflect this by openly advertising for candidates who will preach short, humorous sermons. Many preachers seem themselves to be in full flight from preaching. While they would tell us that they have been "called to preach," they oftentimes seem to not want to preach. Imagine a fisherman not wanting to fish or a golfer not wanting to play golf!

How are we to explain such things? Some say preaching is necessarily in decline because people have shorter attention spans than those of previous generations. Others argue that we live in an entertainment culture. We may not like it, they argue, but it's a fact. Instead of resisting it, we must find ways to go along with it. If we don't, there is no future for the church. And some tell us that preaching was once an accepted mode of communication, but it's now outdated.

The root of the modern distaste for preaching is ignorance. We don't know who God is, who we are, and what the Bible is. Who is God? He is our Maker and our Sustainer, and He will eventually be our Judge. Who are we? We are rebels. We don't live the way our Maker intended us to live, we don't appreciate what He does to sustain us, and we don't concern ourselves with His judgment. What is the Bible? It is God speaking to us about these very issues. It is God telling us the truth about Himself and about us. Moreover, it is God revealing to us the only way that rebels can stand safely before Him when He judges. That way is Jesus, the God-Man, who lived the life we have refused to live and who received on the cross the wrath we deserve.

Knowing these things prompted my doctor in Brazil to express thanks. If you know them, thank God. And while you are at it, thank Him for faithful preachers.

-3-

From God's Word, the Bible...

Moses took his tent and pitched it outside the camp, far from the camp, and called it the tabernacle of meeting. And it came to pass that everyone who sought the LORD went out to the tabernacle of meeting which was outside the camp.

Exodus 33:7

The Tent of Meeting

Here's a very important question: When can we expect to see God moving in extraordinary ways to achieve extraordinary things? Or we can put it this way: When can we expect to see a season of God's mercy and power?

And here, I suggest, is the answer to those questions: when God's people so feel the burden of the times that they are willing to take special measures to seek God's face.

We can find in Moses an example of this answer. Moses certainly felt the burden of his time. He and the people of Israel were camped at the foot of Mt. Sinai. While Moses was on the mount to receive God's laws, the people were cavorting and carousing around a golden calf (Ex. 32).

It was a case of flagrant, full-throttled idolatry deserving of severe judgment. And severe judgment is what Moses meted out. Moses realized that it wasn't enough to eliminate the idol. The people must be encouraged to wholeheartedly turn back to God. So he set up a tent for that purpose. This tent was not the tabernacle, which had not yet been constructed (Ex. 35-40). It was a tent of meeting set up outside the camp, and "everyone who sought the LORD" went out to this tent of meeting.

We may assume that many Israelites, also feeling the burden of their situation, took advantage of this tent of meeting. We know that they had "mourned" when they heard the "grave tidings" that the Lord was withdrawing from them (Ex. 33:1-4). And we know that the tent of meeting achieved its purpose as God promised to be present with His people again (Ex. 33:14).

This episode in the life of Israel should prompt us to ask ourselves some very searching questions. Are we guilty of idolatry? Are we aware how such idolatry grieves God and drives Him from us? Are we taking any special measures to seek God?

If we don't answer the first question in the right way, we can't answer the other questions in the right way. In other words, if we don't see our idolatry, we can't see God withdrawing from us. And if we don't see God as withdrawn, we certainly won't be taking any special measures to seek Him.

We don't seem to be guilty of idolatry. After all, we're not dancing around a golden calf as the Israelites did. But if idolatry is more subtle than blatant, it is still idolatry, and idolatry, whether subtle or blatant, drives God away. The truth is that anything that receives from us the time, the attention, the allegiance, and the love that belong to God alone is idolatry. Anything that keeps us from loving, worshipping, and serving God as we ought is an idol, and every idol grieves God.

Many churches used to have what they called "revival meetings." We know that having a meeting isn't the same thing as having a revival, but it was easier for these churches to say "revival meetings" than to say "meetings to seek revival."

These meetings were intended to be like Moses' tent of meeting. They were intended to call the people of God to go outside the camp to seek God; that is, they were intended to urge God's people to lay aside as much of their ordinary routine as possible and give attention to God.

Such meetings have all but died out. The reason? Church members became increasingly unwilling to lay anything aside so they could seek God. It became clear that church members had become so comfortable inside the camp (their normal lives) that they wouldn't go outside the camp.

Is this a plea for churches to return to having revival meetings? No, it is rather a plea for us to feel the burden of our idolatry and the absence of God. The sad truth is that most Christians have little or no interest in seeking God because they don't even realize that He is missing! As long as the church machinery is running, they assume that God is present with His people and blessing them.

If we have been saved, we would do well to remember that it is because Jesus went outside that camp to die on the cross for us (Heb. 13:12-13). There, the sinless Son of God took upon Himself the sin and disgrace of all who would ever turn from their sin and trust in Him.

-4-

From God's Word, the Bible...

But God, who is rich in mercy, because of His great love with which He loved us, even when we were dead in trespasses, made us alive together with Christ (by grace you have been saved), and raised us up together, and made us sit together in the heavenly places in Christ Jesus, that in the ages to come He might show the exceeding riches of His grace in His kindness toward us in Christ Jesus.

Ephesians 2:4-7

"But God" (1)

Two little words consisting of six letters! But what words! Enfolded in them is our only hope for eternal life in heaven. Those two little words come from the pen of the Apostle Paul. Blessed pen that wrote these blessed words: "But God"!

The first three verses of Ephesians 2 present us with a scene of unrelieved gloom. They place us in a graveyard. Somber place! This is not the typical graveyard with bodies resting beneath the sod and headstones marking the resting places. This is a much sadder graveyard. It is the graveyard of souls. This is the graveyard of spiritual death.

It may seem to be lunacy, but the fact is we are all born into a graveyard. We're born dead. We're living physically, but we're dead spiritually—dead toward God! We come into this world in a state of living death. Physically alive! Spiritually dead!

Why are we in this state? What is it that produces spiritual death? It's all due to sin. Sin has killed us spiritually. It has made us dead toward God. By nature we have no interest in Him. We're not interested in knowing Him. We certainly don't love Him. We have no desire to serve Him.

Do you need proof of your spiritual deadness? Paul supplies it. He tells us to look at the course we follow, the god we obey, and the cravings we fulfill. The answer is plain, isn't it? We follow the course of this world. Just as the water in a river follows the course dictated to it by the riverbed, so we follow the course dictated to us by this world. We think, talk, and act the way the world wants.

We obey the god of this world—Satan. He is the ruler of the invisible kingdom of darkness, a kingdom that permeates this world just as the atmosphere does.

And the cravings we fulfill are those of the flesh. Spiritual deadness so enslaves us to our physical appetites and desires that we find it virtually impossible to say "no" to these things. While we're dead in regard to God, we're very much alive in regard to sin.

This horrible state of spiritual deadness isn't only true of one person here and a few others over there. It's true of all of us. Paul's phrase "even as the rest" (v. 3) could be translated "just like everyone else."

Think of physical death for a minute. While there are degrees of decay among the dead, there are no degrees of deadness. The person who died a hundred years ago is more decayed than the one who died five minutes ago, but they are both equally dead. In the spiritual realm, some sinners are worse than others, that is, they go deeper into sin than others. But a great sinner is no more spiritually dead than other sinners.

Is there any hope for dead sinners? There is! That hope is bound up in those words: "But God."

We're all by nature in the spiritual graveyard, and there we would have stayed were it not for this—God comes into that graveyard and raises the dead. He grants spiritual life to spiritually dead sinners.

Why does He do this? It's certainly not because those spiritually dead sinners do anything to earn it. How can a dead person earn anything? It's rather because God is "rich in mercy" (v. 4). It's "by grace" that we're saved (v. 10).

Would you see the greatness of God's mercy toward dead sinners? You must look to the cross where Jesus died. God's mercy toward us is always channeled through Christ (v. 7). He died that we might live.

"Surely, there is something I must do to earn that grace," says the sinner. Then it's not grace any more. Mix one element of human merit in with God's grace, and you no longer have grace (Rom. 4:4; 11:6).

But doesn't our faith earn salvation for us? No, faith—which is itself the gift of God—merely receives the salvation God provides. The hands of grace are the working hands in salvation while the hands of faith are simply the receiving hands.

I was in the spiritual graveyard, but God brought me out. Let me now go along life's way rejoicing in those two little words—but God!

-5-

From God's Word, the Bible...

But as for you, you meant evil against me; but God meant it for good, in order to bring it about as it is this day, to save many people alive.

Genesis 50:20

"But God" (2)

Quite often in the Bible we find those blessed words "but God." Oftentimes those words put before us dire circumstances from which there seems to be no escape only to have God step in and reverse things.

In the previous reading we rejoiced in the most glorious "but God." We who have been saved were in the spiritual graveyard. We were without spiritual life and without hope. "But God," because of His abounding mercy, found us and gave us life.

The above verse presents us with another thrilling instance of "but God." The instance in the first reading can be called "the 'but God' of salvation or regeneration." The instance before us now can be called "the 'but God' of providence." Yes, we are dealing here with God's providence in the life of one of the Bible's most heroic men—Joseph.

You know about Joseph. Because he was the firstborn son of Jacob's beloved wife Rachel, his father loved him more than he did the sons of his other wives. (No, the Bible doesn't endorse polygamy, but sinful men have often endorsed it.)

Jacob's partiality toward Joseph was so obvious that Joseph's brothers intensely hated him and wanted to be rid of him. One day their opportunity arrived, and they sold him into slavery in Egypt.

In Egypt, Joseph was falsely accused by his master's wife and wrongly imprisoned. Joseph's special ability to interpret dreams finally brought him before Pharaoh, and his skill in interpreting Pharaoh's dream both released him from prison and made him second to Pharaoh in the land of Egypt.

Through a fascinating series of events, Joseph was reconciled to his brothers. He then resettled them and their families, along with their father Jacob, in the land of Egypt. When Jacob died, Joseph's brothers began to vex themselves with the thought that Joseph would at long last get his revenge. But Joseph reassured them with the "but God" of Genesis 50:20. There was a sovereign hand at work in all that had happened. That hand was the hand of God. While God certainly didn't approve of the evil that Joseph's brothers had done to him, He was able to use that evil to further His purposes.

God's providence didn't come to an end with Joseph and his brothers. It lives on. What is God's providence? It is God governing every aspect of everything He has created so that He may achieve His purposes and bring glory to His name. God's providential ordering of things consists of three parts. *General* providence is God sustaining and preserving the created order. *Special* providence is God working in the lives of people. *Extraordinary* providence is God doing the miraculous.

There have been times in which God's people rejoiced in that area of special providence. It brought them tremendous consolation to believe that God was at work in the circumstances of their lives for His glory and for their good. This doesn't appear to me to be one of those times. We have become fixed on our own comfort and ease, and we seem to think God should be equally fixed on it. When something comes along to disturb us or disrupt us, we think God has failed us and we besiege heaven with our "Why?" questions.

Sour circumstances make it very difficult for us to believe that the same hand that so expertly governed the life of Joseph to a good end has lost none of its expertise. The devil is always ready to pronounce on our difficult circumstances as proofs that God doesn't love us and that our faith is vain. He will always make sure we read our difficulties in the most God-adverse manner possible. Meanwhile, God Himself urges us in His Word to trust Him and obey Him. He urges us to reason in this way: Can the God who put His Son on the cross to deliver us from eternal condemnation suddenly turn against us? Is the God who delighted to save us through His Son now finding His delight in making us miserable through hard circumstances? That can never be! The heart of love that sent Jesus has not changed. So when our circumstances are most trying, let's rest in that heart of love and say with Joseph: "…but God…"

-6-

From God's Word, the Bible...

Then Jonathan and David made a covenant, because he loved him as his own soul. And Jonathan took off the robe that was on him and gave it to David, with his armor, even to his sword and his bow and his belt.

1 Samuel 18:3-4

A Deed to Win Your Heart

I definitely have this event in my "Things I Would Like to Have Seen" category. Perhaps the Lord will replay it for me on His celestial video machine.

At first glance, it doesn't appear to be so much. Jonathan pledges his friendship to David. I'm sure many would place it in their "So What?" category.

But look again, and look closer. Here is Jonathan, the son of King Saul and the apparent heir to his throne, declaring himself to be the friend of the man who was perceived by many to be Israel's next king. They should have been rivals! Reason would seem to say that Jonathan should have placed the tip of his sword squarely under David's chin, pressed just hard enough for it to draw a bit of blood, and said: "If you know what's good for you, you will drop any notion of being king. That throne belongs to me!"

But, no, Jonathan doesn't do what reason would seem to dictate. He lays that very sword at David's feet, along with his robe, his armor, his bow, and his belt. This is Jonathan relinquishing his claim to the throne. This is Jonathan pledging his friendship to David. This is Jonathan declaring that he will never be David's enemy, that he will never employ his weapons against him.

Does this mean Jonathan had lost his senses? A royal heir might easily get only one shot at being king, so is Jonathan giving it up? How are we to explain this? It's obvious that David had won Jonathan's heart. What had David done to win his heart? He, David, had slain the giant Goliath, and in doing so had delivered the Israelites from being enslaved by the Philistines. And David had won this victory in the most unlikely way imaginable—with a shepherd's sling and a stone!

The biblical account of Jonathan laying his robe, armor and weapons before David isn't here to extol the virtue of friendship. It isn't here to urge us to try to be friendlier with those we consider to be rivals. It's rather here, as is the case with all biblical accounts, to drive us to Christ.

The Lord Jesus has won for His people a greater victory over a greater enemy than David did. When David came on the scene, the Israelites were facing the prospect of bondage. When Jesus came on the scene, we were already enslaved to Satan (Eph. 2:1-3). We were already part of his miserable dominion (Col. 1:13). The Lord Jesus defeated Satan, freed us from our bondage to him, and brought us into His own kingdom. And Jesus did all this by means of an instrument that would seem to be far more ineffective than David's sling and his stone. The instrument the Lord Jesus used? A Roman cross!

Our sin makes us part of Satan's dominion. It gives Satan the right to hold us in bondage. On the cross, Jesus paid the penalty for all who will believe in Him. He received in the place of sinners the wrath of God against their sins. With that penalty paid, Satan has no right to us any longer and has to let us go.

David became the champion of his people by defeating Goliath. In Christ we have a greater champion because he defeated a greater Goliath, that is, Satan himself.

David's heroic act had won Jonathan's heart. Has the greater act of the Lord Jesus won our hearts?

We can't truly appreciate Jonathan's attitude toward David if we don't compare it to that of his father Saul. Even though the Lord was clearly at work in David for the benefit of the entire kingdom, Saul never gave his heart to David. There was no room in Saul's heart for anything or anyone except himself.

The Bible calls each of us to lay before Christ our robe of self as well as our armor and weapons of sin. We can respond to Jesus as Jonathan did to David, or we can emulate Saul by wrapping ourselves more tightly in the robe of self and clutching more firmly the weapons of sin. Saul's opposition to David didn't turn out well, and neither will opposition to the Lord Jesus.

-7-

From God's Word, the Bible...

He sends the springs into the valleys;
They flow among the hills.
They give drink to every beast of the field;
The wild donkeys quench their thirst.
By them the birds of the heavens have their home;
They sing among the branches.
He waters the hills from His upper chambers;
The earth is satisfied with the fruit of Your works.

Psalm 104:10-13.

Gone to the Birds

Some time ago I was asked to preach in a Bible Conference for Laurel Creek Baptist Church in East Tennessee. Through the years it has been my privilege and pleasure to preach in many country churches. So I went with the expectation that this church would be like many others. I was in for a pleasant surprise. The services were very well attended. The building was very close to being full for four out of the five services. But the thing that really got my attention was the singing of those people. How they sang! I shall never forget their triumphant, glorious singing of these words:

> *My sin, oh, the bliss of this glorious thought —*
> *My sin — not in part, but the whole —*
> *Is nailed to the cross and I bear it no more,*
> *Praise the Lord, praise the Lord, O my soul!*

We've all heard it said that something or someone has "gone to the dogs." I would say those dear folks had "gone to the birds." They had, as it were, taken their places as pupils and let the birds teach them. Martin Luther once said: "…we have as many teachers and preachers as there are little birds in the air."[2]

In Matthew 6, Jesus used the birds to tell us that those who trust in God need not worry and fret. But the psalmist points to the bird to teach another lesson, that is, the importance of singing praises to God.

Psalm 104 is a psalm of praise. It is a psalm that celebrates the greatness of God. Notice how it begins:

> *Bless the LORD, O my soul!*
> *O LORD my God, You are very great:*
> *You are clothed with honor and majesty…*

From that initial burst of praise, the psalmist proceeds to celebrate the marvels of God's work of creation. As he works his way through creative wonder after creative wonder, he finally comes to the springs of water from which the animals drink. He says of these springs:

> *By them the birds of the heavens have their habitation;*
> *They sing among the branches.*

Perhaps the psalmist still had the singing of the birds on his mind as he began wrapping up the psalm, (v. 33):

> *I will sing to the LORD as long as I live;*
> *I will sing praise to my God while I have my being.*

Christians are to be God's singing people. Why? I can give you some God-oriented answers: because God com-

---

[2] Martin Luther (1521), *The Sermon on the Mount*, translated by Jaroslav Pelikan, Vol 21 of *Luther's Works* (Concordia 1956), pp197-8.

mands it (Ps. 95:1-2; 96:1-2; 100:1-2; 146:1-2; 147:1,7; 148:1-4; 149:1,5; 150:1-6), enjoys, it and deserves it.

I can also give you a devil-oriented answer: we should sing because the devil hates to hear us offering praise to our God. It stands to reason. If he hates God, and he certainly does, he has to hate praise to God. So if you want to make the devil sick, sing!

I can also give you an unbeliever-oriented answer: our singing (if it is loud and triumphant and not muffled and mealy-mouthed) can arrest the attention of those who aren't Christians and convince them that they urgently need the Christ who makes us sing. Many people live without a reason to sing. Our singing can't help but make an impression on them.

Although these are very compelling reasons, the distressing fact is many of us don't sing as we should. We focus on our inability instead of our responsibility, that is, if we can't sing well, we think we shouldn't sing at all. We think of reasons we shouldn't sing instead of reasons we should. When that is the case, we need to go to Bird School. We should let the birds' singing remind us to sing.

I see myself now in Bird School. Mr. Bird asks: "Why are you here?" And I respond: "I'm hoping you can help me improve in my offering praise to God." And Mr. Bird says: "The best help I can give you is to send you to another school. It is called 'Cross School.'"

Mr. Bird has made his point. While it's okay for me to look at the birds and let them remind me to sing, my greatest need is always to look at the cross of Christ, where Jesus died for sinners like you and me. If that doesn't make me sing, nothing will.

-8-

From God's Word, the Bible...

So the eunuch answered Philip and said, "I ask you, of whom does the prophet say this, of himself or of some other man?" Then Philip opened his mouth, and beginning at this Scripture, preached Jesus to him.

Acts 8:34-35

A Good Meeting

It occurs to me that a good bit of my life has been taken up with meetings of various kinds. I've been involved in lots and lots of meetings—some good, some not so good. Some things are essential for a good meeting. There must be attendees. There's no meeting if no one shows up. There should be an agenda. And something should be achieved.

In Acts 8:26-39, Luke (the author of Acts) describes for us a good meeting. He tells us about *the attendees*. There were two men. One was a man who is not named. He is only identified as "a man of Ethiopia, a eunuch of great authority" (v. 27). The other was Philip, who is first mentioned in Acts 6:1-6 and earlier in this eighth chapter of Acts (vv. 4-8).

Two men were present? Yes. But another person was present as well—the Holy Spirit. It was He who arranged this meeting. He had been working on both sides to make this meeting occur—on the Ethiopian's side and on Philip's side.

The Ethiopian was returning to his homeland from Jerusalem. He had been there to worship God. Why would a man from Ethiopia go all the way to Jerusalem for that purpose? The Ethiopians surely had their own gods. Yes, but this particular man wasn't satisfied with those gods. So he went to Jerusalem, but he wasn't satisfied there either. Searching he came to Jerusalem, and still searching he headed for home.

How are we to explain the yearning and disillusionment of this man? The Spirit of God was behind it, preparing this Ethiopian for the most profound discovery of his life.

The Spirit also worked on Philip's side. After an angel instructed Philip to take the road that ran from Jerusalem to Gaza (v. 26), the Spirit took over and commanded Philip to overtake the chariot in which the Ethiopian was riding (v. 29). Through this process, we see Philip as a ready and obedient participant. Let's learn from him to desire and work toward being instruments of the Lord.

That brings us to *the agenda* for this meeting.

As he traveled along, the Ethiopian was reading from the fifty-third chapter of Isaiah's prophecy. When Philip asked if he understood what he was reading, the Ethiopian admitted his bewilderment. Was the prophet speaking of himself or of someone else? Philip knew the answer. It was Jesus of whom Isaiah was speaking. Isaiah 53 is a prophecy of the Messiah, and the Lord Jesus is the Messiah. More to the point, Isaiah 53 is a prophecy of the Messiah dying for sinners, and Jesus died for all sinners who will believe in Him and His redeeming work.

What happy words are these: "Then Philip opened his mouth, and beginning at this Scripture, preached Jesus to him" (v. 35).

So the Holy Spirit made sure that Jesus was the agenda

for this meeting. If Jesus is on the agenda, and He is accurately presented, the meeting can't help but be good.

This account of Philip comes as a stirring reminder that the business of the church is to preach Jesus. When the Ethiopian asked Philip about whom the prophet was writing, Philip didn't say: "Never mind this prophecy. Let me ask you how you are doing as a family man." Nor did he say: "I will share with you some principles for managing your finances and give you some insights into developing a more forceful personality."

That is the type of thing the church today is often saying, but it is most emphatically not what Philip said.

The final component of this meeting is *the achievement*. There have been lots and lots of meetings that didn't accomplish anything, but the Holy Spirit made sure this meeting was productive. The Ethiopian was saved. Philip urged him to believe in Jesus with all of his heart, and he, the Ethiopian, responded: "I believe that Jesus Christ is the Son of God" (v. 37). And he gave evidence of his conversion to Christ by submitting to baptism (v. 38).

What a good meeting this was—an Ethiopian, Philip and the Holy Spirit! What a good agenda—Jesus! And what a good outcome—conversion!

Because this was such a good meeting, all of us who know Christ will enjoy another good meeting. We will get to meet the Ethiopian in heaven.

-9-

From God's Word, the Bible...

But the following night the Lord stood by him and said, "Be of good cheer, Paul; for as you have testified for Me in Jerusalem, so you must also bear witness at Rome."
And when it was day, some of the Jews banded together and bound themselves under an oath, saying that they would neither eat nor drink till they had killed Paul.

Acts 23:11-12

Bright Truths for Bleak Times

It was a bleak time for Paul. Roman soldiers had taken him into custody to prevent his fellow-Jews from killing him. But that didn't put an end to it. Forty of the Jews took an oath they would neither eat nor drink until they had killed Paul (v.14). They went to their religious leaders with a plan, and those men, who professed to be great believers in God's law, put their stamp of approval on it.

Was this a difficult time for Paul? I would say so. But there is more here than the description of hard circumstances. Interwoven into this account are four bright, encouraging truths.

First, we see that *no place is too hard for the Lord to find*.

After arresting Paul, the Romans put him "into the barracks" (v. 10). Paul may have been alone there, hidden from human view. Ah, but, he wasn't hidden from the Lord's view because we read: "the Lord stood by him" (v. 11). The religious leaders in the temple and the Roman commander in the palace were surrounded by comfort while Paul was in prison surrounded by the Lord. I'd say Paul had the better of it. It's better to be in a prison with Christ than to be in a palace without Him.

Do you feel as if you are hidden away in harsh circumstances? The same Lord who knew where to find Paul knows where to find you. He is with His people in every difficulty and every trial. When the Jews were captives in Babylon, they thought their situation was hidden from the Lord, but it wasn't (Isa. 40:27). And neither is ours.

A second bright truth is this: *No thought is too deep for the Lord to know.*

The forty conspirators, and the religious leaders who were cheering them on, thought that they had thrown a cloak of secrecy over their plan. But the Lord knew all about it.

Hostility toward God and His people is so prevalent today that we may find ourselves worrying about the future. What plans are being hatched against us by evil men? We may not know. It is enough that the Lord knows.

There's tremendous comfort in the Lord's knowledge. He not only knew what the Paul-haters were planning but He also knew it even before those evil men themselves knew it. The knowledge of God is perfect knowledge. He knows the wicked plans of wicked men, and He knows the anxieties and fears, the heartaches and heartbreaks His people endure in evil times.

Here is the third bright truth: *No person is too small for God to use.*

The evil plan is in place. The evil planners are secure in their belief that Paul's life is as good as over. One small detail changes everything. Big doors turn on small hinges! That small detail is Paul's nephew. Somehow he learns about the conspiracy, and he informs Paul and the Roman commander (vv. 16-22).

Paul's nephew! What was his name? We don't know. He emerges from obscurity to play a pivotal role in this whole affair and then goes back into obscurity. We have never met him before in Scripture, and we never meet him again. He could very well have been a common, ordinary fellow. But on this occasion the Lord used him.

We may think that we are too small or too ordinary for God to use, but that's never the case. God has always delighted in using ordinary things (David and his sling, Samson and his jawbone, the lad and his lunch, for example) to achieve extraordinary things.

What is the final bright truth in this passage? It is a glorious one: *No enemy is too great for the Lord to defeat.*

The conspiracy was strong, but God was stronger. He got Paul out of Jerusalem and to Rome, just as He had promised (v. 11).

Let Paul represent the gospel of Christ, and the forty men opposition to that gospel. Hatred of the gospel has been so intense that it has often seemed that it could not survive. But it will never die. Let the devil and his minions rage and conspire, no plot formed against God and His gospel can prosper.

Are these bleak times? Yes. But no amount of bleakness in this world can override or nullify these bright truths. Thank God!

-10-

From God's Word, the Bible...

But when the kindness and the love of God our Savior toward man appeared, not by works of righteousness which we have done, but according to His mercy He saved us, through the washing of regeneration and renewing of the Holy Spirit, whom He poured out on us abundantly through Jesus Christ our Savior, that having been justified by His grace we should become heirs according to the hope of eternal life.

Titus 3:4-5

Today Thy Mercy Calls Us

In my circles, the hymn *Today Thy Mercy Calls Us* falls into one of two categories: never discovered or almost forgotten. That's regrettable because it is a truly splendid hymn.

I can't tell you much about its author, Oswald Allen. He was born in England in 1816. His father, John Allen, was a banker. Oswald himself would also make banking his career. But he was also a devoted Christian and a hymn writer. In addition to authoring several hymns, Oswald published *Hymns of the Christian Life* in 1861. He died on October 2, 1878.

I can tell you that each verse throbs with encouragement, comfort and hope. Read and savor verses one and two:

Today Thy mercy calls us to wash away our sin.
However great our trespass, whatever we have been,
However long from mercy our hearts have turned away,
Thy precious blood can cleanse us and make us white today.

Today Thy gate is open, and all who enter in
Shall find a Father's welcome and pardon for their sin.
The past shall be forgotten, a present joy be given,
A future grace be promised, a glorious crown in heaven.

Several words in those verses seem to wave their arms at me and say: "Look at me!" The first of those words is *mercy*. It is, as the hymn's title indicates, the dominant theme in the hymn. What is mercy? It is showing compassion and kindness to an enemy or offender over whom we have power.

Someone has deeply offended or injured me. I have every right to punish, but I choose to forego that and show compassion instead. That is mercy.

It is, of course, God's mercy that Allen's hymn is celebrating. Here is the truth of the matter—we have deeply offended God by our sins. He has the perfect right to punish us with that punishment that He has pronounced on sinners, that is, eternal separation from Himself. But instead of exercising that right, He shows mercy.

How can God show mercy to sinners? Doesn't His justice demand that the penalty be carried out to the utmost? Does God show mercy by setting aside His justice? If He does so, isn't justice itself deeply offended?

The answer to those questions lies in another word that calls urgently for attention. It is the word *blood*, and that refers to the Lord Jesus Christ shedding His blood on the cross. That blood satisfied the claims of God's justice. It meant that there on the cross Jesus was taking the penalty that sinners deserve. When justice was satisfied, the way was cleared for God to show mercy to sinners. Justice demands that the penalty for sin be paid only once—not twice. If Jesus paid it for the sinner, there is nothing left for that sinner to pay.

In regard to all sinners who believe in Jesus, God has said

to His justice: "Hush, and put your sword away. Jesus has died."

With the voice of justice silenced by Jesus, mercy can call to sinners to believe in Jesus. And it does call. Have you heard its call?

Perhaps you are thinking that there can be no mercy for you because you have been too great a sinner. You can and should rejoice in more words that cry for attention: *However great our trespass, whatever we have been.*

There's no such thing as too great a sinner. No one is a greater sinner than Jesus is a Savior. The Lord Jesus never says: "I can save this person because he's not much of a sinner, but I can't save that person over there because he's too much of a sinner." What kind of Savior would Jesus be if He could only save some sinners?

Are you wondering if you are hearing mercy's call? If you can say you want your sins forgiven and to be right with God, you may be assured that God's mercy is calling you. Thank God that you are hearing that call, and throw yourself on Jesus.

One more word from Allen's first verse should get our attention. It is the word *Today*. Mercy is calling today. So receive it today, and be thankful that it is great enough to cover all your sins.

-11-

From God's Word, the Bible...

I will make them and the places all around My hill a blessing; and I will cause showers to come down in their season; there shall be showers of blessing.

Ezekiel 34:26

Drops and Showers

The small country church in which I spent my childhood years would often sing the hymn of Daniel Whittle (1840-1901), *There Shall Be Showers of Blessing*. I recall that some would invariably add an "s" to "blessing," but it is one blessing with which the song deals. What is that blessing? It is the revival of God's people.

God's people often find themselves lacking in vitality and vigor. They can and do decline in their spiritual health. Some would have us believe that a graph of the Christian's experience would show a straight line steadily angling upward, but most of us know that such a graph would have to consist of a wavy line. Christians are sometimes up and sometimes down in their spirituality, and it can be amazing how low they can sink in their down times. The sad truth is that spiritual lowness often becomes widespread. It's not just a Christian here and there who is declining. It's rather a matter of most declining. And their decline involves both what they believe, and how they behave—that is, they become shaky in their convictions and cozy with both sins of commission and omission—doing things God has told them not to do and failing to do those things that He has told them to do.

In such times, God's people need revival. What is revival? It is God's people being brought back to spiritual health and vitality. It's a season in which God's people experience substantial improvement in their spiritual condition. Apathy and indifference are replaced with interest and zeal. Sins are abandoned, relationships are restored, church services are packed, people are saved—all of these and more happen when God sends the glorious blessing of revival to His people.

Here is the chorus of Whittle's hymn:

> *Showers of blessing,*
> *Showers of blessing we need:*
> *Mercy drops round us are falling,*
> *But for the showers we plead.*

I remember wondering about those "mercy drops." I eventually came to understand those drops to mean that God sends blessings even when most of His people are in a very unhealthy state. We are never totally without expressions of His mercy. When the gospel of Christ is accurately and powerfully preached, that is a mercy drop. When someone is saved, that is a mercy drop. When an individual Christian sees his or her decline and draws near the Lord again, that is a mercy drop.

In times of widespread spiritual decline, we should always be thankful for mercy drops. How precious they are! But we should never be satisfied with them. My assessment is that today's church is so content with the mercy drops that she is not pleading for the showers. We are satisfied with the trickle when we need the torrent.

Whittle encourages us to plead for those showers. He tells us in the first verse that God has promised to send "seasons refreshing," and he urges us in the third verse to pray:

> *Send them upon us, O Lord;*
> *Grant to us now a refreshing,*
> *Come, and now honor Thy Word.*

Are we praying for revival? Are we pleading with God for it? Can we identify with these lines from Whittle's fourth verse:

> *There shall be showers of blessing:*
> *Oh, that today they might fall....*

We can't make revival happen, but we can more earnestly desire it, and a more earnest desire may very well mean that it is actually beginning. We can begin to plead, but we will not plead until we see our need.

In the days of Elijah, the people of Israel were suffering from the physical drought God had sent. That drought was the result of a spiritual drought that had been in place for a very long time. The physical drought was God's punishment for the people turning from Him to serve idols. God used Elijah to break the spiritual drought and the physical drought. In the breaking of the latter, Elijah said to King Ahab: "... there is the sound of the abundance of rain" (1 Kings 18:41).

Let's be thankful for mercy drops, but let's plead for the showers of revival and keep pleading for them until we can say: "... there is the sound of the abundance of rain."

> *Oh, that today they might fall....*

-12-

From God's Word, the Bible...

Now Naaman, commander of the army of the king of Syria, was a great and honorable man in the eyes of his master, because by him the LORD had given victory to Syria. He was also a mighty man of valor, but a leper.

2 Kings 5:1

A Great Man

If a survey had been conducted to name the cool characters in ancient Syria, Naaman might very well have been most frequently mentioned. He was the coolest of characters. Commander of the Syrian army, brave and strong, highly regarded by the king, respected and admired by his countrymen—this was Naaman.

Naaman seemed to have the world by the tail, and he loved that world. It had given him wealth, success, and standing. It had checked all his boxes. Naaman knew how to move around in his world. He knew how to make things happen. He knew how to get things done.

As we read this verse, we might find ourselves expecting it to end with the words "and he lived happily ever after." Instead it ends with these five heavy words: "but he was a leper."

Now there was an ugly fly in Naaman's ointment, a monkey wrench in his gears, a dark cloud in his sky, a horrible clang in his melody, and an upset for his apple cart.

Leprosy was the most dreaded disease of Naaman's time.

It consisted of the slow eating away of the flesh until death came. It also meant living apart from others. Every part of this disease had to be repulsive to Naaman, but being isolated from the Syria he loved so much might have been the part that repulsed him the most.

When we first meet Naaman, he had apparently not yet arrived at the stage that would require his isolation. He was still moving around, but he knew isolation must come.

Now Naaman was getting a new angle on things. He was proud of himself, and he was proud of Syria. But his horrible leprosy made it clear that he couldn't help himself and his beloved Syria couldn't help him either.

Sick and helpless! What a strange and unfamiliar set of circumstances for Naaman!

Have you ever wondered why the Holy Spirit wanted this account included in the Bible? Is it possible that it was to serve as a mirror? Is the Holy Spirit holding Naaman before us so we can see ourselves? Are we to see ourselves in his love for life in this world? Are we to see ourselves in the way he proudly went along as if this life is all that matters? Are we to see ourselves in his smug assurance that his views on culture, life and religion were superior? Yes, I think so. But there's a more basic and essential seeing of ourselves in this Naaman mirror. We're to see in his leprosy our own more dreadful and deadly disease. Naaman's disease would eventually eat his flesh down to his bones. Our disease eats into our minds, our affections and our wills, darkening the first, degrading the second, and deadening the third.

Our disease is sin, and it truly is "our" disease. No one is exempt from it (Rom. 3:23). We are born with a sinful nature, and it doesn't take long for that nature to manifest itself in sinful words and deeds.

What is sin? It's refusing to live in accordance with the laws of the God who made us. Why is it serious? The God who made us will eventually be our judge. The God whose laws we have spurned will finally call us to account (Rom. 14:12; Heb. 9:27). And our law breaking will finally lead to death—eternal death, that is, eternal separation from the very God against whom we have rebelled.

Yes, sin is serious!

Can anything be done about our sin disease? The Bible answers with a thundering "Yes!" There was, as we shall see, a cure for Naaman, and there is a cure for sinners. Naaman's cure didn't come from himself or from Syria. It came from God. It is the same with our sin disease. The cure comes from God, and it comes in the form of His Son, the Lord Jesus Christ.

To those who object to the Bible affirming that Jesus is the only cure for our sin disease, I ask: "How many cures do we need?" I didn't reject the only cure because there weren't a dozen cures. I was glad for the one and accepted it by repenting of my sins and trusting in the Lord Jesus Christ.

-13-

From God's Word, the Bible...

And the Syrians had gone out on raids, and had brought back captive a young girl from the land of Israel. She waited on Naaman's wife. Then she said to her mistress, "If only my master were with the prophet who is in Samaria! For he would heal him of his leprosy."

2 Kings 5:2-3

A Young Girl

Naaman, the great man, had a great problem—leprosy! His bright sky was now darkened with despair. All he had ahead of him was a slow, agonizing death—or so it would seem.

Suddenly and quite unexpectedly, there was a bright beam of hope that shot across his dark sky. It came from an enslaved girl. One of Naaman's raiding parties had made a foray into Israel. This young girl was one of the tokens of their success. Cruelly ripped away from her home, she was now a servant of Naaman's wife.

When she learned about the leprosy of Naaman, she pointed out that "the prophet who is in Samaria" could heal him. That prophet was Elisha.

This young girl was a marvel. She was a blend of contentment, concern, and confidence.

Her *contentment* must surely amaze us. She could have been filled with bitterness about her circumstances. She could have even been angry with God for allowing those circumstances to come her way. But here she was accepting her circumstances and speaking about God. Yes, in speaking of Elisha, the man of God, she was speaking about God.

Christians are called to speak for God, but many of us are tongue-tied. Two things that tie our tongues are difficult circumstances and disappointment with God. We can't recommend God to others if we are angry with Him.

We also see *concern* in this young woman. She was concerned about the condition of Naaman. What an amazing thing! She could have secretly rejoiced in Naaman's leprosy and kept Elisha's name to herself, but she genuinely desired the best for her master.

Concern for others is the lifeblood of witnessing for Christ. Are we who know Christ genuinely concerned for those who don't know Him? Have we lost sight of the fact that each person in this world is bound for another world—the eternal world—and that faith in Christ is the only way to enter safely into that world?

Finally, we see her *confidence*. This girl would never have said what she did were it not for her confidence that she really possessed the answer for Naaman's problem. Consider her words: "If only my master were with the prophet who is in Samaria! For he would heal him of his leprosy."

We find no hesitation or doubt in her words. She could have said: "There is a possibility that my master might be healed by the prophet." But she didn't hedge or equivocate. She didn't know any doubt because she knew the God of Israel and how He was working through the prophet Elisha.

Many today would call her bigoted and dogmatic and would condemn her for trying to impose her beliefs on others. They would point out that the Syrians had their own religion, and she had no right to suggest that her religion was superior.

I get the impression that this young girl wouldn't have been fazed in the least by such charges. I think she would have been glad to say with the apostles Peter and John: "...we cannot but speak the things which we have seen and heard" (Acts 4:20).

She saw a need, she knew the answer, and she didn't concern herself with what others might think or say.

One reason so many Christians are silent about their faith these days is they lack confidence in the very message that they should believe with all their hearts. There is a lack of triumphant certainty among us. The language of the early church featured the words "We know." We prefer to use these phrases: "We think," "We believe," "We suggest."

In his sermons, the evangelist Vance Havner used to diagnose our problem in this way: "We believe that there is some darkness in our light and some light in the world's darkness."

This young girl helped Naaman. She also helps us. She calls us to be content with our circumstances, concerned about others, and to be supremely confident in the gospel, saying with Paul: "For I am not ashamed of the gospel of Christ, for it is the power of God to salvation, for everyone who believes..." (Rom. 1:16).

-14-

From God's Word, the Bible...

...Then the king of Syria said, "Go now, and I will send a letter to the king of Israel." So he departed and took with him ten talents of silver, six thousand shekels of gold, and ten changes of clothing. Then he brought the letter to the king of Israel, which said, Now be advised, when this letter comes to you, that I have sent Naaman my servant to you, that you may heal him of his leprosy. And it happened, when the king of Israel read the letter, that he tore his clothes and said, "Am I God, to kill and make alive, that this man sends a man to me to heal him of his leprosy? Therefore please consider, and see how he seeks a quarrel with me." So it was, when Elisha the man of God heard that the king of Israel had torn his clothes, that he sent to the king, saying, "Why have you torn your clothes? Please let him come to me, and he shall know that there is a prophet in Israel."

From 2 Kings 5:4-8

Mr. False Assumptions

The message for Naaman from the servant girl in his house was clear and unmistakable—Go to Elisha the prophet in Israel and be healed of leprosy (v. 3).

So we might expect to read that Naaman headed to Samaria, found the prophet, and received the cure. It might have been very simple had Naaman's king, the King of Syria, stayed out of the matter. But he interjected himself in two ways. First, he loaded Naaman down with silver, gold and garments (as implied in verse 5). Then he sent a letter along with Naaman to the King of Israel in which he stated that he was expecting the King of Israel to cure Naaman (v. 6).

With Naaman outside his door, the King of Israel was reading and reeling, that is, reading the letter and reeling with distress. How could he, the King of Israel, cure a man of leprosy? Was the King of Syria trying to provoke a quarrel?

We might call these kings the movers and shakers of their day, with the Syrian king doing the moving and the Israelite king the shaking.

At this point, two questions press upon us. The first is why the king of Syria filled Naaman's chariots with goods. The second is why he sent along the letter demanding that the king of Israel heal Naaman.

In each case the Syrian king was falsely assuming something. He sent the treasures because he falsely assumed that the cure could not be free. He sent the letter because he falsely assumed that the prophet Elisha worked for the king of Israel. The Syrian king had his own prophets, and he assumed that it was the same in Israel. If a prophet in Israel had the cure, that prophet must work for the king of Israel! So if the prophet worked for the king, it was six of one and a half dozen of the other as to who would actually do the healing.

The Syrian king had no category for a man like Elisha. Yes, the prophet worked for a king—not the king of Israel—but the King of Kings, that is, the Lord God Himself.

The treasure the Syrian king sent was based on a false assumption, as was the letter he sent. Let's just call the Syrian king "Mr. False Assumptions."

Mr. False Assumptions died centuries ago, but his descendants are still among us. The earth is well populated with them.

The Bible talks about the reality of our sin and the severity of it, but Mr. False Assumptions rejects that teaching out of hand because he assumes that we are all basically good.

The Bible's great theme is forgiveness for our sins through faith in the Lord Jesus Christ and His redeeming work on the cross. But Mr. False Assumptions merely dismisses it. Why? He assumes that if we really do need forgiveness for our sins, it is ludicrous beyond measure to believe that such forgiveness could come through a man dying on a cross.

In addition to telling us that the Lord Jesus provided salvation for sinners, the Bible says that there is nothing we can do to earn or deserve that salvation. It is the gift of God's grace. And how does Mr. False Assumptions respond? He tells us that he believes if we try to live a good life we will go to heaven when we die. And old hymn says:

> *Nothing in my hand I bring;*
> *Simply to Thy cross I cling.*

Mr. False Assumptions goes along singing:

> *Something in my hand I bring –*
> *My own goodness, and to that I cling.*

The truth that looms large before us at this point is quite plain. As long as the Syrian king, Mr. False Assumptions, was occupying center stage, there was no cure for Naaman. There he sat outside the palace door of the King of Israel still in his leprosy. There was no cure for him until Elisha occupied center stage. And there is no cure for our sins until we rid ourselves of our false assumptions and let Jesus Christ occupy center stage. Our hope for salvation lies not in man and his wisdom. Rather, it lies in saying with Jeremiah:

> *Heal me, O Lord, and I shall be healed;*
> *Save me, and I shall be saved…*
> (Jer. 17:14)

-15-

From God's Word, the Bible...

So he turned and went away in a rage. And his servants came near and spoke to him, and said, "My father, if the prophet had told you to do something great, would you not have done it? How much more then, when he says to you, 'Wash, and be clean'?" So he went down and dipped seven times in the Jordan, according to the saying of the man of God; and his flesh was restored like the flesh of a little child, and he was clean.

And he returned to the man of God, he and all his aides, and came and stood before him; and he said, "Indeed, now I know that there is no God in all the earth, except in Israel; now therefore, please take a gift from your servant."

From 2 Kings 5:9-15

Clean

It must have been an impressive sight—Naaman in his splendor with his retinue of servants and his chariots laden with silver, gold and garments.

Elisha didn't even bother to come out and look. The chariots of earth held little appeal for the one who had been dazzled by the chariot of heaven (2 Kings 2:11-12).

Naaman came to Elisha with more than shimmering silver and glittering gold. He came with expectations. Like his boss, the King of Syria, Naaman had false assumptions. If his king was Mr. False Assumptions, Naaman was Mr. False Assumptions, Jr.

It's plain that Naaman wasn't content to merely receive the cure from Elisha. He wanted Elisha to cure him in a certain way. How eager we are to dictate to God the way that He should do things! Lots of us want to serve God—as advisers!

What did Naaman expect? He wanted Elisha to come out and meet him and, in so doing, show him great respect and deference. Perhaps Elisha would ask him for his autograph!

Then Elisha would perform a religious ceremony. He would "wave his hand over the place, and heal the leprosy" (v. 11).

It was not to be. Elisha didn't come out at all. He wasn't interested in Naaman's greatness. He didn't want his autograph. He merely sent out the message that Naaman was to "wash in the Jordan seven times" (v. 10).

Naaman was furious! Elisha's "cure" offended him. It was too humbling. A man of his standing must bathe in the muddy waters of the Jordan? It was preposterous! Here is the truly preposterous thing—an unclean man objecting to bathing in an unclean river!

Now it was time for Naaman's servants to step in and reason with him. Are we beginning to understand that Naaman was not the central character in this drama? It was God. While He was scarcely mentioned at all, God was at work. It was God who prompted the servant girl's testimony (v. 2). It was God who caused Elisha to take control of the situation (v. 8). And it was God who now moved Naaman's servants to speak to him.

These men employed simple logic. Leprosy was such a serious disease that any possibility of a cure had to be embraced. If the prophet had asked Naaman to do a difficult thing, he would have attempted it. How much more should he be willing to embrace a simple cure (v. 13)!

So Naaman did as Elisha commanded. Six times he immersed himself in the muddy waters of the Jordan, and nothing happened. But in full compliance with Elisha's command, Naaman took a seventh dip and came up a healed man. What blessed words are these: "and he was clean" (v. 14)!

Naaman immediately made his way back to Elisha to offer the testimony that there is only one God, the God of Israel (v. 15).

At this point, we see the point. All of this happened, not

so much to heal Naaman of his leprosy, but rather to bring him to true faith in God, and to give glory to God.

Just as Elisha directed Naaman to do something of a repulsive nature, so God directs us to do something repulsive for the healing of our sin. God tells us to kneel in repentance and faith before the cross of Christ.

That cross repels us. It doesn't live up to our standards. In His infinite wisdom, God has determined that His plan of salvation will not satisfy man's wisdom (1 Cor. 1:21). The world looks at the cross of Christ and cries, "Foolishness!" But even God's foolishness is much wiser than the greatest wisdom men can ever generate (1 Cor. 1:25).

It doesn't appear now that God's foolish cross will actually prove to be His wisdom, but eternity will eventually tell the tale. An innumerable multitude of saved sinners will gather around God's throne to offer praise for Christ's "foolish" death on the cross (Rev. 5:9). Then the whole universe will know that death was not so foolish after all.

The choice before us is either to reject the crucified Christ so we can be considered wise by this foolish world or to receive the crucified Christ so we can be considered wise by the "foolish" God. When we stop rebelling against the cross, what was said of Naaman will be said of us: "and he [or she] was clean."

-16-

From God's Word, the Bible...

But Gehazi, the servant of Elisha the man of God, said, "Look, my master has spared Naaman this Syrian, while not receiving from his hands what he brought; but as the LORD lives, I will run after him and take something from him."

2 Kings 5:20

Where is My Heart?

Gehazi was an unusually blessed man. Very few have enjoyed anything comparable to the privileges that came his way. He was chosen by Elisha the prophet to be his servant. Elisha was no ordinary prophet. He was a miracle-working prophet. The most notable of Elisha's many miracles consisted of him raising a young man from the dead. Gehazi had a front row seat on that occasion (2 Kings 4:8-37).

It was another of Elisha's miracles, the healing of Naaman, that led to Gehazi's downfall.

Naaman had come to Elisha's house with enormous wealth, thinking that he would make Elisha wealthy if Elisha would only make him healthy.

But Elisha, uninterested in Naaman's wealth, flatly refused to accept a single shekel (vv. 15-16). Elisha wanted one truth to stand out in solitary grandeur in Naaman's mind—the healing he received was the gift of God's marvelous grace. It was something that had no connection with human merit.

Gehazi was there to observe Naaman's offer and Elisha's refusal. How those Syrian coins must have gleamed and glittered before his eyes! How appealing must the garments have seemed! How he must have winced when Elisha sent Naaman away!

Not sharing his master's view of things, Gehazi caught up with Naaman. He pretended that Elisha had experienced a change of heart and would now be happy to take some of Naaman's goods (v. 22).

But Gehazi wasn't expressing Elisha's heart. He was expressing his own. He was revealing that his heart was in Syria. Israel was the nation that God had chosen to put the truth of His saving grace on display, and at this time Elisha was the man God had chosen to be the foremost spokesman for that grace. But as he stood there looking at Naaman's silver, gold, and garments, Gehazi must have realized that his heart wasn't in Israel and with the prophet Elisha. It wasn't in what God's grace and power could do for a man. It was rather in what Syria could do for that man. Gehazi's body was in Israel, but his heart was in Syria.

Gehazi asks each of us to ask himself: Where is my heart? Is it in God and His gracious plan of salvation for sinners? Or is it in the fleeting and fading things of this world? Many these days seem to be Israelites, but they are actually Syrians. They profess to know God, but their hearts are not in worshiping Him or obeying Him. Their hearts are in the things of this world. Yes, they will have religion as long as they can think, talk, and act like the world. But tell them that they cannot have both, and they will choose the world.

Gehazi also speaks to pastors and churches who exist to declare God's gospel of grace. He asks them to ask themselves: *Are our hearts really in the gospel?* Those who insist on presenting Christianity as nothing more than a successful living technique have given us their answer.

Gehazi should have known that his plan wouldn't work. He had been associated with Elisha long enough to know that the prophet was in touch with the God from whom nothing is hidden.

Sure enough, when Gehazi returned from his ill-conceived venture, Elisha was waiting for him with a devastating announcement. The leprosy of Naaman was to cling to Gehazi and his descendants (v. 27).

The severe temporal judgment that befell Gehazi serves as a miniature picture of the eternal judgment that will eventually befall all those who deny God's gospel of grace.

In chasing after Naaman, Gehazi experienced an awful and wonderful moment of self-knowledge. It was awful because it showed him that his heart was far from God and the truth of God's grace. But it was also wonderful for this reason: in seeing his heart was far from God, he, Gehazi, could turn to God in true repentance and faith.

We should hope that the temporal judgment that befell Gehazi was the means that God used to bring him to his senses and to keep him from experiencing far worse judgment in eternity. And we should also hope that his story will be used by the Lord to help us know where our hearts are. Gehazi saw more riches in Naaman's gold than in God's grace. Now he warns us to not do the same.

Is your heart where the gospel would have it to be? Are you trusting in Christ alone? The call of Proverbs 23:26 is to all believers: "My son, give me your heart."

-17-

From God's Word, the Bible...

He who is faithful in what is least is faithful also in much; and he who is unjust in what is least is unjust also in much.

Luke 16:10

Buying Bread

In his book *I Give You Glory, O God*, Jerry Bridges relates an experience that powerfully riveted an important truth in his mind. He and his wife had gone to a small, specialty bakery to buy bread. They had with them a two for the price of one coupon. When they presented it to the salesclerk along with their two loaves of bread, she explained that the coupon was only good at their new bakery that was opening that day. Although that wasn't indicated on the coupon itself, Jerry and his wife agreeably complied by returning their second loaf to the shelf.

Much to their surprise, the clerk thanked them for being so kind and understanding. They soon learned that several customers had berated her that morning when they learned that the special deal didn't apply in that store.

Jerry Bridges and his wife didn't treat her that way. They acted as Christians ought to act. As Jerry and his wife talked about the experience, it occurred to him that Christians are always on duty even in such simple matters as buying bread.

Always on duty! That's the Christian. He or she must not take time off from being a Christian. There is no holiday, no vacation or no sabbatical in our Christianity. We're on duty when we speak. We're on duty when we're alone with our thoughts. We're on duty when we're with people we know and when we're with people we don't know. We're on duty when we're with people who deserve to be treated kindly and when we're with people who don't. We're on duty when we open the doors of our houses to go out into the world, and we're on duty when we close those doors to be with our families.

Sometimes it easier to act like a Christian in the face of life's big things than it is in the face of life's little things. A family is suddenly stricken with tragedy, and we make sure we are there to offer comfort and assistance. That's good, very good. But what about the clerk in the bread store? How have we treated her or him?

The truth is that we can be faithful in large things and fail to be in little things. But if we are faithful in the little things, we can be sure that we will be faithful in the large things.

Jesus is, of course, our example in this matter of always being on duty. He never took a break from living for the honor of His Father and for the glory of His name. He never gave way to irritability and short-temperedness. When a large multitude intruded on a time that He had set aside for rest for Himself and His disciples, there was not a trace of anger or irritability in Jesus. To the contrary, when Jesus saw the "great multitude," He was "moved with compassion for them, because they were like sheep not having a shepherd" (Mark 6:34).

On another occasion, Jesus' disciples may have showed some irritability when people began bringing their children to Jesus. But Jesus said: "Let the little children come to Me, and do not forbid them…" (Matt. 19:13-14).

Even on the cross, Jesus refused to lash out with anger but rather prayed: "Father, forgive them, for they do not know what they do" (Luke 23:34).

In these instances and in every instance from the life of Jesus, He was "leaving us an example" so that we "should follow in His steps" (1 Peter 2:21).

I will add my own word of testimony. I can say that I have never regretted any time that I acted as a Christian. I have always regretted those times in which I didn't.

On March 6, 2016, Jerry Bridges finished his earthly journey and entered the presence of his Lord. I can imagine the Lord receiving him with these words: "Well done, good and faithful servant." I can also imagine Jerry asking: "Lord, are you referring to the books I wrote?" And it wouldn't surprise me if the Lord responded: "No. I'm referring to the time you were buying bread."

-18-

From God's Word, the Bible...

But Naomi said, "Turn back, my daughters; why will you go with me? Are there still sons in my womb, that they may be your husbands? Turn back, my daughters, go—for I am too old to have a husband. If I should say I have hope, if I should have a husband tonight and should also bear sons, would you wait for them till they were grown? Would you restrain yourselves from having husbands? No, my daughters; for it grieves me very much for your sakes that the hand of the LORD has gone out against me!"

Ruth 1:11-13

Come and Go

People often say odd things. One coach had this to say to his players: "Two words summarize this sport—you never know."

Yogi Berra offered this observation on baseball: "Ninety per cent of this game is half mental."

Odd words come from those who either don't think or can't think.

In Ruth 1, we have Naomi saying a very odd thing again and again. It must have been because she didn't really stop to think about what she was saying.

I'm talking about what she said to her daughters-in-law. As she was preparing to leave Moab and go back to her home in Bethlehem, Naomi told Ruth and Orpah to stay in Moab. This was not merely a suggestion from Naomi. This was urging. This was persuasion. In verse 8, she says to them: "Go, return each to her mother's house." In verse 11, she says to them: "Turn back, my daughters; why will you go with me?" In verse 12, she says: "Turn back, my daughters, go your way."

Orpah finally did as Naomi asked. She turned and walked away. Now alone with Ruth, Naomi said: "Look, your sister-in-law has gone back to her people and to her gods; return after your sister-in-law" (v.15).

This doesn't seem to be such a big deal. Naomi is going back to Israel, and she wants her daughters-in-law to stay in their homeland. Why make a fuss about it? Here's the answer: Orpah had decided to turn back "to her gods," and Naomi urges Ruth to do the same.

Naomi was from Israel, and Israel was the nation to whom God had revealed Himself and His gracious plan of salvation. When Orpah and Ruth express their desire to go to Israel, Naomi tells them to go back to their gods! What a shocking thing for an Israelite to say! She tells them to turn away from Israel where they could find the true knowledge of God and stay with their false gods in Moab.

There's only one way to explain it. While Naomi herself believed in the God of Israel, she was a backslider, and backsliders say and do strange things.

The truth is that Naomi shouldn't have been in Moab at all. She, her husband Elimelech, and their two sons had left Israel when a famine set in. That wasn't the right thing for them to do. The people of Israel were in a special covenant relationship with God. The land itself was part of that covenant. If the Israelites lived in faithfulness to God, the land would be fruitful. If they didn't, the Lord might send a famine to correct them (Lev. 26:14-29; Deut. 28:15-24).

The proper response to such a famine was spiritual in nature. It lay in the people honestly confronting their sins and seeking God's forgiveness. It was not to leave the land (Deut. 30:8-11).

The choice of Elimelech and Naomi to leave the land was, therefore, a choice to not be part of the solution. It was an indication that their hearts had strayed from the Lord.

They were backsliders, a fact that Naomi herself admitted when she spoke of the Lord's chastisement (Ruth 1:20-21).

I can't help but compare the words of Naomi to Ruth and Orpah to the words Moses spoke to his brother-in-law, Hobab. "Come with us," Moses said, "and we will treat you well; for the LORD has promised good things to Israel" (Num. 10:29).

"Go," said Naomi. "Come," said Moses. Naomi was wrong; Moses was right.

Ruth refused to be persuaded by Naomi. We might say the Lord's persuasion was more powerful than Naomi's, leading Ruth to say:

> *Entreat me not to leave you,*
> *Or to turn back from following after you;*
> *For wherever you go, I will go;*
> *And wherever you lodge, I will lodge;*
> *Your people shall be my people,*
> *And your God, my God.*
> (Ruth 1:16)

We should also note that Jesus has a "come" and "go" of His own. Regarding the matter of knowing God in this life, the Lord Jesus, unlike Naomi, always says "come" and never "go." It doesn't matter how sinful we may have been, the Lord Jesus always says: "Come" (Matt. 11:28).

But if we go through this life rejecting His invitation to come to Him in repentance and faith, we will eventually hear Him say: "Go" (Matt. 7:23).

-19-

From God's Word, the Bible...

...praying always with all prayer and supplication in the Spirit, being watchful to this end with all perseverance and supplication for all the saints...

Ephesians 6:18

Prayer: Important and Difficult

In my years of walking with the Lord, I've become convinced of two things regarding prayer:
- Nothing is more important;
- Nothing is harder.

We surely don't need to be persuaded about the importance of prayer. That truth is prominently displayed in the Bible. I've never attempted to count them, but it has been said that there are 650 prayers in the Bible. A total of 650—that's a lot!

The Bible also emphasizes the importance of prayer by telling us that the greatest heroes of the faith prayed: Abraham, Moses, Elijah, David, Paul—they were all men of prayer.

The Apostle Paul often stressed the importance of prayer. He writes to Timothy: "Therefore I exhort first of all that supplications, prayers, intercessions, and giving of thanks be made for all men..." (1 Tim. 2:1). The phrase "first of all" means "as a matter of first importance."

Paul also urged the church in Colosse to "continue earnestly in prayer" (Col. 4:2). And to the church in Thessalonica, he says: "Pray without ceasing" (1 Thess. 5:17).

While prayer is prominently displayed in the Bible, it is particularly displayed in the life of Jesus. If anyone would seem to have needed not to pray, it was Jesus, who was fully God and fully man. But pray Jesus did. Luke tells us that he prayed often (5:16) and, on at least one occasion, all night (6:12). He also makes note of Jesus praying on other occasions (9:28; 11:1; 22:41). Furthermore, Luke tells us that Jesus taught his disciples to pray (11:1-4). On another occasion, Jesus shared a parable to drive home the point that "men always ought to pray and not lose heart" (Luke 18:1).

What a lesson there is in this! If Jesus thought it necessary to pray, how much more should we!

In light of the emphasis the Bible puts on prayer we can't doubt its importance. We rather have to agree with these words from J.C. Ryle: "Prayer is the very life-breath of true Christianity."[3]

But prayer—real prayer—isn't easy. True prayer isn't merely repeating without feeling the same few phrases we've used over the years. True prayer is coming to God the Father on the basis of the redeeming work of Jesus and in the power of the Holy Spirit to express worship, confession, and thanksgiving and to make our requests known.

Why do we find prayer to be so difficult? One answer is that the devil, knowing far better than we the importance and value of prayer, strives mightily to hinder us in our praying. Some of the Puritans used to say that the devil "fetches a mischief against us" when we pray.

We tend to think that the church must move forward through programs, promotions and personalities. The devil

---

[3] J.C. Ryle *Expository Thoughts on Luke*, The Banner of Truth Trust, vol. ii, p.253.

fears none of these. He knows that if the church is to move forward it will be on her knees. So he trembles when we get on our knees.

Another reason that prayer is difficult can be found in ourselves. As Pogo said: "We have met the enemy, and he is us."

I'm saying prayer is hard work, and we are naturally inclined to seek our own ease and comfort.

To these we can add yet another reason prayer is hard for us: it often seems to accomplish nothing at all.

It ought to be enough for us that the Lord wants us to pray! We may not be able to put a finger on anything that prayer is accomplishing. We may not be able to identify an answer. But let us keep on praying because the Lord Jesus desires that we do so.

And of this we may be assured: if we keep on praying, we will eventually find that prayer accomplished far more than we ever thought possible. Our problem is always thinking we see the whole picture and that we are, therefore, in a position to pronounce outcomes. But the truth is that we see only a tiny part of the picture, and the part we see is never sufficient for us to be pronouncing on prayer or any other part of God's working.

Prayer is both important and difficult. The question before each of us is whether we will let the importance outweigh the difficulty or the difficulty outweigh the importance.

-20-

From God's Word, the Bible...

O You who hear prayer,
To You all flesh will come.

Psalm 65:2

Things That Help Me Pray: Loading up on the Privilege

Where is your eye when you pray? I'm talking about your spiritual eye. In other words, what are you looking at when you pray? Are you looking at the duty of prayer—*I know I'm supposed to do this, so I might as well get it out of the way?*

Or are you looking at the privilege? Look at the duty, and prayer will be drudgery. Look at the privilege, and prayer will be a delight.

I see the privilege of prayer in terms of two poles—a north pole and a south pole, if you will. God is one pole and I the other.

Think about God. You and I have never in our best moments ever come anywhere near a true and adequate conception of the greatness, the grandeur, and the glory of God. He is the eternal God without beginning or end. He is the

God who has made all things and who rules over all things. He is the object of the adoration and worship of countless numbers of angels. He is the God of the "omnis"—omniscient (all-knowing), omnipotent (all-powerful) and omnipresent (present everywhere). God is self-existent, self-sufficient, and sovereign. He is righteous, just and holy. He is gracious and good. He is kind and merciful. And God is immutable. That means He is unchanging. He is at this moment all the things that I have mentioned, and He will be all those things tomorrow and forever.

And with all that, we have only scratched the surface. God is greater than our greatest thought of Him. Theologians can't explain Him. Scientists can't observe Him. Poets, painters, and musicians can't capture or express Him. All of them together are like children playing on the shore of the surging ocean, totally unaware of the vast depths beyond.

So there is one of the poles of prayer. And I—and you—are the other pole. Did I liken the privilege of prayer to the North Pole and the South Pole? Those two poles are 12,430 miles apart. But the distance between God and us is immeasurable.

That distance is great if we speak of it only in terms of God the Creator and of man the creature. It is infinitely greater if we speak of it in terms of the Holy God and sinful man. How vast is that gap!

Here, then, is the privilege of prayer. It spans the gap between God and man, the gap between heaven and earth. I can talk to the God who is so far and so incomprehensibly beyond me. I can speak here on earth and be heard in heaven!

God hearing the prayers of His people would be privilege enough, but it goes beyond that. God also delights in those prayers. Just as doting parents delight in the babbling of their infants, so God delights in the prayers of His people.

God's delight is such that He keeps those prayers. He stores them in bowls (Rev. 5:8). Those prayers are never lost. When we get home to heaven, we will find that our prayers are already there ahead of us.

Many suffer these days from the culture of the celebrity. They are fascinated by celebrities from the world of entertainment and/or the world of sports. They would consider it an immense honor if they could speak a few words to one of their celebrities, and if that celebrity would take a mere moment to really listen. The celebrities of this day are to God as a speck of dust is to a mountain, as a teaspoon of water is to an ocean, and as the light of a match is to the sun. If we were to regard it as a privilege to speak to a mere celebrity, how much more should we regard it as a privilege to speak to God?

If we're to pray as we ought, we must load up on the privilege of prayer, that is, think much about that privilege. The more we focus on it, the more we will delight in prayer and the more we will find ourselves singing with Fanny J. Crosby:

> *Blessed hour of prayer,*
> *Blessed hour of prayer,*
> *What a balm for the weary,*
> *Oh, how sweet to be there!*

-21-

From God's Word, the Bible...

For you were bought at a price; therefore glorify God in your body and in your spirit, which are God's.

You were bought at a price; do not become slaves of men.

1 Corinthians 6:20; 7:23

Things That Help Me Pray: Loading up on the Purchase

I have never found it easy to pray. Almost anything in the Christian life is easier for me than really laying hold of God in genuine prayer. I'm always in need of help when it comes to this most vital work.

I have tried to learn how to help myself in praying. One thing I've learned is to load up on the privilege of prayer, that is, to fill my mind with the fact that I, a weak, undeserving sinner, can actually be heard in heaven. I can have the ear of the sovereign, majestic God!

Another thing that helps me to pray as I ought is to load up on the purchase. Every Christian surely knows what I'm talking about. There is one great purchase as far as the Christian is concerned. That is Christ purchasing us by the shedding of His blood on the cross.

It comes down to this for me—the more I think about

what the Lord Jesus Christ did for me on the cross, the more I feel like praying.

I sometimes think that we rob ourselves of real appreciation for what Jesus did on that cross by not personalizing what He did there. The floodgates of joy, gratitude and praise are opened in my mind and heart when I stop to ponder that Jesus died for me. Jerry Bridges puts it this way:

> There was a period in my early Christian life when my concept of God's love was little more than a logical deduction: God loves the world; I am a part of the world; therefore, God loves me. It was as if God's love were a big umbrella to protect us all from His judgment against sin, and I was under the umbrella along with thousands of other people. There was nothing particularly personal about it. Then one day I realized, "God loves me! Christ died for me. [4]

I also think we rob ourselves of deep appreciation for what Jesus did on that cross by thinking of His death in physical terms only. Yes, Jesus died physically, and death by crucifixion was as horrible a death as there could be. But it was not the physical aspect of His death that saves us. It was not the mere fact that He was crucified that saves us. Lots of men were crucified in those days.

We will never appreciate Jesus' death to the degree that we should if we don't understand that it was a special death. Jesus, a special man (the God-man), died a special death because of a special arrangement with God the Father. That special arrangement was this: God the Father would pour out on His Son the wrath that I deserve for my sins. The thing

---

[4] Jerry Bridges, *The Practice of Godliness*. NavPress: Colorado Springs, CO, 1983, p. 32.

that made the death of Jesus so special is that He actually took an eternity's worth of wrath for my sins.

Through my sin I had essentially sold myself out to the penalty for my sin, the wrath of God. But when Jesus took that wrath in my place, He paid that penalty. He paid my debt and purchased me from sin and God's wrath. Now I can happily take as my own the words of Philip Bliss:

> *I will sing of my Redeemer,*
> *And His wondrous love to me;*
> *On the cruel cross He suffered,*
> *From the curse to set me free.*
> *Sing, oh, sing of my Redeemer,*
> *With His blood He purchased me,*
> *On the cross He sealed my pardon,*
> *Paid the debt, and made me free.*
>
> *I will tell the wondrous story,*
> *How my lost estate to save,*
> *In His boundless love and mercy,*
> *He the ransom freely gave.*
> *I will praise my dear Redeemer,*
> *His triumphant pow'r I'll tell,*
> *How the victory He giveth*
> *Over sin, and death, and hell.*
>
> *I will sing of my Redeemer,*
> *And His heav'nly love to me;*
> *He from death to life hath brought me,*
> *Son of God with Him to be.*

Purchased by Christ on the cross? My debt paid? Redeemed from wrath? As I load my mind and heart with Christ on the cross in my place, prayer doesn't seem quite so difficult,

-22-

From God's Word, the Bible...

Praise the LORD!
Praise, O servants of the LORD,
Praise the name of the LORD!
Blessed be the name of the LORD
From this time forth and forevermore!
From the rising of the sun to its going down
The LORD's name is to be praised.

Psalm 113:1-3

Things That Help Me Pray: Loading Up on Praise

I have never met a Christian who thought prayer was unimportant. I have never met a Christian who thought he or she had mastered prayer. I have also never met a believer who disagreed with my assessment that nothing the Christian is asked to do is harder than praying.

I am far from having mastered prayer, but I have discovered over the years that I am helped in my praying if I load up on some things. It helps me to load up on the privilege of prayer and on the price the Lord Jesus paid for me on the cross.

Today, I'm adding a third thing that helps me pray, namely, praise. I try to load up on praise because praise helps me pray. The more I praise God in my praying, the more I feel like praying. Praise primes the pump of prayer. I have found it to be so, and I think you will find it to be so as well.

How does praise help us to pray? First, *it warms our hearts toward God* as we think about who God is and what He has done for us.

It's impossible to pray from a cold heart, that is, a heart that is cold toward God. Sadly enough, our hearts are constantly bent toward coldness. Just try to pray from a cold heart and see how far you get. But praising God causes the coldness to melt away and warmth to come in.

It's not mere coincidence that the Bible puts so much emphasis on praise. The Bible mentions praising God approximately 250 times, with 130 of those occurring in the book of Psalms.

How very much we have for which to praise God! We have past blessings, present blessings, and glorious promises of future blessings. We have temporal blessings (those that pertain to life in this world), and we have spiritual blessings. We have obvious and open blessings (those that are very apparent to us), and we have hidden or disguised blessings (those circumstances in which God is working for our good even when we can't see or discern it). We have daily blessings and special seasons of blessings.

We consider every blessing to be good, and every good thing comes from God (James 1:17).

Praise helps us pray in a second way. *It gives us perspective on our needs.* As we think about who God is and what He has done, we begin to realize that He is more than sufficient to meet our needs. Our needs begin to shrink to their proper size when we place them alongside the greatness of God. In praising God, we find help for our needs before we ever get to our needs.

An example of this is found in Acts 4. The early church was in deep trouble. Peter and John had been threatened and told not to preach in the name of Jesus (Acts 4:17-21).

When they were released, they told their fellow believers about the threat, and the first response of those believers was to pray. But notice how they began their prayer: "Lord, you are God, who made heaven and earth and the sea, and all that is in them…" (Acts 4.24).

Their praying began with God rather than with the trouble, and in beginning with God they found help for their trouble.

So I lay it down as a fundamental rule of praying that we should always begin with praise to God and worship of God. This is what Jesus taught His disciples when He gave them what is known as The Lord's Prayer. My view is that it would be more correct to call it "The Model Prayer." No, Jesus didn't give them this prayer with the intent that they should only say those words every time they prayed and nothing else. This prayer set before them a pattern for prayer or principles for prayer.

As we look at this pattern, we see that it begins with praise:

Our Father in heaven,
Hallowed be Your name.
(Matt. 6:9b)

The prayer also ends with praise:

For Yours is the kingdom and the power and the glory forever.
Amen.
(Matt. 6:13b)

If Jesus filled The Model Prayer with praise, we should fill our prayers with praise. The more we do, the more delight we shall find in prayer.

-23-

From God's Word, the Bible...

Now this is the confidence that we have in Him, that if we ask anything according to His will, He hears us. And if we know that He hears us, whatever we ask, we know that we have the petitions that we have asked of Him.

1 John 5:14-15

Things That Help Me Pray: Lightening the Load

Loading up on certain things helps me to pray. It helps me to fill my mind with the privilege of prayer, with the price Jesus paid for me on the cross, and with praise to God. It also helps me to pray if I lighten my load. It sounds like a contradiction, but it isn't. To pray well means we must load up on those things that help us, and unload those things that hinder us.

One thing we often load ourselves down with is unanswered prayer. We think of instances in which we specifically asked God to do some good thing for us or to keep some evil thing from us, and the good thing didn't happen but the evil thing did.

Because we didn't get what we asked for, we have soured on prayer. We think it does little or no good. We have loaded ourselves down with the problem of unanswered prayer. That is heavy baggage indeed, and we will pray very little or very poorly as long as we carry it.

So we need to think through this business of unanswered prayer. We correctly assume that prayer consists of equal parts of wisdom and power. Someone must know what needs to be done. That's the wisdom part. And someone must be able to do what needs to be done. That's the power part.

Our grand blunder is to think that we supply the wisdom part and God supplies the power part. We would never openly admit it, but we think we know what God ought to do in our lives. So we go to God in our wisdom to ask Him to supply the power, that is, to ask Him to do what we want done.

In doing this, we refuse to grant to God the prerogatives that we reserve for ourselves in parenting. No good parent will say: "My child supplies the wisdom part, and I supply the power part." In other words, no wise parent will do whatever his or her child wants him or her to do.

Every good parent has the best interests of the child at heart. With that being the case, the parent sometimes answers "Yes" to what the child asks. Sometimes, for reasons the child may not understand, the parent answers "No." Does the parent only have the best interest of his child in view when he or she says "Yes"? Does a "No" mean the parent has suddenly lost his or her concern for the child? Not at all! The "No" comes from the same heart of love as the "Yes." And sometimes, the parent answers with a "Not now," and that answer also comes from the same heart of love. In each case, the parent is exercising wisdom in determining what is best for the child.

God is wiser than the wisest human parent. Sometimes God answers our prayers with "Yes." But sometimes He answers with "No" or "Not now." But with each answer, it is God who is supplying the wisdom. He knows what we need, what we don't need and when to give us what we need.

We need to mind our own business on this matter of prayer. Our business is not to fret over our prayers seeming to be unanswered. Our business is to pray. I sometimes think that this is the most important passage in the Bible on the matter of unanswered prayer:

> *Lord, my heart is not haughty,*
> *Nor my eyes lofty.*
> *Neither do I concern myself with great matters,*
> *Nor with things too profound for me.*
> *Surely I have calmed and quieted my soul...*
> (Ps. 131:1-2a)

Some imagine themselves storming into the presence of God to ask: "Why didn't you give me all the things that I asked for?"

They will certainly be surprised to hear God respond: "Why didn't you ask Me for all the things that I wanted to give?" (James 4:2).

We need to concern ourselves much more with the unasked prayer than with the unanswered prayer. And when we finally come into the glory of His presence, we will most surely discover that our unanswered prayers were not really unanswered after all. And we will further discover that those circumstances which we considered to be lapses in God's wisdom were, in fact, part of His wisdom.

-24-

From God's Word, the Bible...

Then He spoke a parable to them, that men always ought to pray and not lose heart, saying: "There was in a certain city a judge who did not fear God nor regard man. Now there was a widow in that city; and she came to him, saying, 'Get justice for me from my adversary.' And he would not for a while; but afterward he said within himself, 'Though I do not fear God nor regard man, yet because this widow troubles me I will avenge her, lest by her continual coming she weary me.'"
Then the Lord said, "Hear what the unjust judge said. And shall God not avenge His own elect who cry out day and night to Him, though He bears long with them? I tell you that He will avenge them speedily. Nevertheless, when the Son of Man comes, will He really find faith on the earth?"

Luke 18:1-8

Keep on Praying!

Have you lost heart in prayer? To keep His disciples from losing heart in prayer, Jesus gave them a parable. Because we easily lose heart in praying, we need this parable as much or more than they.

Jesus' parable features a woman who was in dire need. Her husband had died. That was calamity enough in those days. But this woman had even more on her plate. She had "an adversary" (v. 3). Someone had done something to make her life very difficult. Perhaps this person had swindled her out of the little money she had. Or perhaps he had prevented her from receiving something to which she was entitled.

Whatever the nature of the misdeed, this woman quite obviously had a legitimate legal claim. She went to the judge in her city pleading: "Avenge me of my adversary." (v. 3).

She was asking for justice, but this judge had no concern for justice. He was "a judge who did not fear God nor regard man" (v. 2).

What was this poor woman to do? She had asked and nothing had happened. If anyone could be excused for losing heart, it was she.

But she refused to give up. She decided to make a pest of herself until this judge took action and gave her the ruling she needed. It wasn't because he suddenly took an interest in justice. No, he was exactly the same man that he had been before. It was just to get this woman out of his life.

Jesus made the application by raising this question: "And shall God not avenge His own elect who cry out day and night to Him, though He bears long with them?" (v. 7).

He then supplies the answer: "I tell you that He will avenge them speedily" (v. 7).

The point of the parable is very plain. If an unjust judge could be persuaded by persistence to do something for someone he did not care about, how much more can God be persuaded by the persistence of those whom He cares deeply about!

How do we know God cares for His people? There's a world of meaning in that word "elect" (v. 7). God's people are His people because he set His love on them even before the world began and chose to redeem them through His Son (Eph. 1:3-4).

Because God, unlike the judge in this parable, is kind and caring, prayer is not overcoming His reluctance but rather seizing on His willingness.

But if God cares so deeply and is so eager to answer, why do we have the problem of unanswered prayer?

Much of our problem stems from having a different view or understanding of prayer than God. We have a tendency to view it exclusively as a way to get things from God. Whatever we want and when we want!

But God has not appointed prayer as the means for only giving us things. It is also one of the ways in which He trains us.

Is it not true that parents do the same with their children?

Do they not use the requests of their children as opportunities for training them? God, the wise Father, gives to us in much the same way as wise parents give to their children. We do not give our children everything for which they ask, because they sometimes ask for things that are not good for them. They sometimes ask in the wrong way. They sometimes ask after they have been particularly sullen, ungrateful, and disobedient. And we sometimes let them ask more than once so they will have greater appreciation for the gift when it comes. That which is too easily gained is not usually highly prized!

We are far too casual in prayer already. Think about how casual we would be if we were given everything for which we ask as soon as we ask!

Of this we may be assured: if we keep on praying, we will eventually find that prayer accomplished far more than we ever thought possible. Our problem is always thinking we see the whole picture and that we are, therefore, in a position to pronounce. But the truth is that we see only a tiny part of the picture, and the part we see is never sufficient for us to be pronouncing on prayer or any other part of God's working.

Let's ever be mindful in our praying that people all around us need the Lord. They need to see their sins and their coming judgment. They need to be pointed to the Lord Jesus Christ who came to this earth and went to the cross to provide forgiveness for sinners. And we need to pray that the Holy Spirit will enable people far and wide to lay hold of the gospel in true faith. If we've been doing such praying, let's keep on. If we haven't, let's start.

-25-

From God's Word, the Bible...

*Seek the LORD while He may be found,
Call upon Him while He is near.
Let the wicked forsake his way,
And the unrighteous man his thoughts;
Let him return to the LORD,
And He will have mercy on him;
And to our God,
For He will abundantly pardon.*

Isaiah 55:6-7

"Help, I Have Done Awful Things!"

The devil wants to keep unbelievers from coming to faith in Christ and believers from serving Christ. He often uses the same argument with each. To the unbeliever, he says: "You're too bad to be saved." To the believer, he says: "You're too bad to serve."

The answer is the same in each situation. God's grace is greater than our sins. God can save the most stained sinner. God can restore the most soiled saint.

Let's call the roll of some of the very worst sinners. King Manasseh of Judah sacrificed his own sons to idols. But Manasseh was forgiven. Saul of Tarsus was a ferocious persecutor of the church. But Saul was saved and became the Apostle Paul, the foremost preacher of the church. Augustine was deeply entrenched in sin, but he was saved. John Newton was one of the most disgusting and vile reprobates who ever came along, but Newton was saved and became the author of the hymn *Amazing Grace*.

And God hasn't used up His grace in saving such men. His grace constantly renews itself. There is as much of it today as there has ever been. There's enough for you. One of the most frequent responses I've received from people as I've presented the gospel is this: "If you only knew what I've done, you wouldn't say that I can be forgiven."

I do say it. You are not a greater sinner than Christ is the great Savior.

And what about soiled saints? Yes, every saint is soiled in some way. Christians aren't perfect in this life. Perfection comes later. Let's call the roll of a few of those soiled saints. Noah got drunk (Gen. 9:20-23), Abraham lied about his wife (Gen. 12:10-20; 20:1-18), Moses lost his temper (Num. 20:7-11), and David committed adultery and murder (2 Sam. 11:1-27).

Then we fast forward to the New Testament, and we immediately think of Simon Peter. Given the opportunity to stand up and speak up for the Lord Jesus, Peter failed. He denied the Lord—not once, not twice, but three times!

There was so much Peter could have said about the Lord. When he was accused of being one of Jesus' disciples, Peter could have said: "Yes, I'm one of His disciples and proudly so. I've seen Him open the eyes of the blind and the ears of the deaf. I've seen Him make the lame to walk and the mute to speak. I've seen Him cast out demons, still storms, and feed multitudes. I've even seen Him raise three people from the dead."

Yes, that and a thousand other things is what Peter could have said, but, alas, he did not. He denied Christ. Denial would have been bad enough in and of itself, but Peter denied in a very shocking and vehement way. He wasn't content to merely say: "You must have me confused with someone else." The Gospel of Matthew tells us that he even laced his denials with cursing (Matt. 26:74).

But there was forgiveness for Simon Peter. The very Lord that he had denied sought him out and asked him three times if he, Simon, loved Him. And each time Simon Peter answered: "Yes." How gracious of the Lord to give Simon the opportunity to reverse each one of those nasty denials (John 21:15-19)!

When we as Christians fall into sin, the devil always wants us to debate within ourselves whether God can forgive. While the devil calls us to debate whether forgiveness is available, the Lord calls us to delight in it and to avail ourselves of it. He assures us that He casts our sins behind His back, not to be seen again, and casts them as far from us as the east is from the west, never to be remembered again.

When the devil says to us: "You have sinned. You must stop serving the Lord," we need to hear the words of Samuel to the people of Israel: "Do not fear. You have done all this wickedness; yet do not turn aside from following the LORD, but serve the LORD with all your heart" (1 Sam. 12:20).

Stained sinners and soiled saints are all called to rejoice in God's forgiving grace.

Grace, grace, God's grace,
Grace that will pardon and cleanse within;
Grace, grace, God's grace,
Grace that is greater than all our sin!
(Julia H. Johnston)

-26-

From God's Word, the Bible...

You are of purer eyes than to behold evil,
And cannot look on wickedness.
Why do You look on those who deal treacherously,
And hold Your tongue when the wicked devours
A person more righteous than he?
Though the fig tree may not blossom,
Nor fruit be on the vines;
Though the labor of the olive may fail,
And the fields yield no food;
Though the flock may be cut off from the fold,
And there be no herd in the stalls —
Yet I will rejoice in the LORD,
I will joy in the God of my salvation.

Habakkuk 1:13; 3:17-18

"Help, I'm Disappointed with God!"

We know about disappointments. We expect something to turn out a certain way, and it doesn't. So we're disappointed.

A lot of people wouldn't hesitate to say that they are disappointed with God. They believe that He has failed them in some way. Perhaps He appeared to break a promise, seemed to not answer their prayers, didn't protect them from hardship or didn't appear to prosper the work that they did for Him. Or it may be that they simply have not experienced in the Christian life what they expected to experience, that is, they haven't felt God's presence, haven't experienced joy in serving Him, or haven't found strength for facing life's difficulties.

Disappointment with God isn't a new thing. It has been in existence for a very long time, and some of the greatest people in the Bible experienced it. Job was disappointed that God let him suffer although he had lived righteously. Jonah was disappointed that God didn't judge the Ninevites. Mary and Martha were disappointed that Jesus didn't come to heal their brother before he died. Paul must have been disappointed that God didn't remove his thorn in the flesh.

And here we have Habakkuk. He was disappointed that God was planning to use the Babylonians to bring judgment upon the Jews when they, the Babylonians, were the more sinful of the two.

What are we to do when we are disappointed with God? *We should begin by checking our expectations.* We often want to obligate God to do things that He has never obligated Himself to do. God has never promised that He will exempt His people from trials and difficulties. As a matter of fact, He has said the opposite (Acts 14:22; 2 Tim. 3:12; 1 Peter 4:12).

If we insist on believing that God's purpose is to make life easy for us, we are going to be constantly disappointed with Him. God has made us to know, love, serve, trust, and glorify Him. With those things as His purpose, we may be sure that He is going to do things quite differently than He would if our ease were His purpose.

After we get our expectations in order, *we must learn to delight ourselves in God.* That is the big lesson we learn from Habakkuk. He began with being disappointed with God, but he came out in a good place (Hab. 3:17-19).

How did Habakkuk get to this good place? It wasn't because his situation suddenly changed. His people were still sinful, and God was still planning to use the more sinful Babylonians as His instrument of judgment. It was because Habakkuk made the deliberate decision to draw his joy from God rather than from his circumstances.

We find the Apostle Paul doing the same. Even though

he was imprisoned, Paul made the determination that he would rejoice in the Lord (Phil. 1:18; 4:4).

Habakkuk and Paul determined to draw their joy from God because they understood that they had nothing without God. We would do well to learn from them. In the midst of our disappointments and frustrations, we are to delight ourselves in God. We certainly don't have all the answers with Him, but we have no answers without Him. Think about it for a moment. Take God out of the equation, and we still have our disappointments and sorrows, but without God we have nothing else. It's better to have those disappointments and sorrows with God than to have them without Him.

What does it mean to delight ourselves in God? It means delighting in those things that God Himself delights in: His perfections (Jer. 9:23-24), His Son (Isa. 42:1; Matt. 3:17), His Son's redeeming death (Isa. 53:10), His Word (Ps. 138:2), His day (Isa. 58:13-14), public worship (Ps. 149:1,4), prayer (Prov. 15:8), and obedience (1 Sam. 15:22-23).

Another thing for us to do when we are disappointed with God is look to our future. Disappointments aren't permanent for God's people. If God doesn't ease them for us in this life, He most certainly will in the life to come. In heaven there will be no disappointments.

If we want to get to that land of no disappointments, we must repent of our sins and trust the Lord Jesus Christ and in His atoning work. Those who come to God through Christ will not be disappointed because God never fails to save the sinner who trusts in Christ.

-27-

From God's Word, the Bible...

Then He said to Thomas, "Reach your finger here, and look at My hands; and reach your hand here, and put it into My side. Do not be unbelieving, but believing."
And Thomas answered and said to Him, "My Lord and my God!"

John 20:27-28

"Help, I Find It Hard to Believe!"

Christianity offers the most indescribably glorious benefits imaginable. It tells us that we can have forgiveness for our sins and right standing with God on the basis of what the Lord Jesus Christ has done. It further tells us that all who repent of their sins and believe in Christ have eternal life awaiting them in a world that is free from pain, sorrow and death.

Many would like to believe this message, but they find it hard to do so for several reasons:

- these things sound to good to be true
- an overwhelming majority appear to reject these things
- many of those who claim to believe these things live as if they don't really believe them
- many other religions make conflicting claims
- many highly intelligent people reject Christianity.

Put Thomas, one of Jesus' original twelve disciples, into the category of those who find it hard to believe. He was asked to believe something that seemed impossible, namely, that Jesus had risen from the dead. This was such a staggering claim that it did indeed seem too good to be true.

But Thomas should have believed in the resurrection of Jesus. He had more than sufficient reasons for doing so. He was present on those occasions when Jesus predicted His resurrection (Matt. 16:21; 17:22-23; 20:17-19). He had seen Jesus raise three people from the dead (Mark 5:35-43; Luke 7:11-17; John 11:38-44). And the testimony he heard about Jesus' resurrection came from ten men whom he, Thomas, knew to be completely dependable and trustworthy.

Thomas was not asked, therefore, to believe for no reason, but rather to believe on the basis of sufficient reasons. He wasn't called to make a leap of faith into the dark with the unfounded hope that all would turn out well.

But with these sufficient reasons in hand, Thomas refused to believe. With sufficient evidence, he demanded total evidence: "Unless I see in His hands the nails, and put my finger into the print of the nails, and put my hand into His side, I will not believe" (v. 25).

Eight days after Thomas made his emphatic statement, the risen Lord suddenly appeared. After greeting all of His disciples (v. 26), the Lord directly addressed Thomas: "Reach you finger here, and look at My hands; and reach your hand here, and put it into My side. Do not be unbelieving but believing" (v. 27).

Isn't it amazing that Jesus was so kind and tender toward Thomas? His doubt deserved a severe reprimand, but Jesus' reprimand was more encouraging than severe.

Thomas wasn't rebuked because he had refused to believe without any reasons but rather because he refused to believe with more than enough reasons. He wasn't rebuked because he refused to take a blind leap of faith but rather because he refused to believe on the basis of inescapable reasons.

Thomas didn't carry out his plan to touch the nail prints and to place his hand in Jesus' wounded side. Hearing Jesus quote his own words was sufficient for him to abandon his doubt. When Thomas heard those words, he realized that the risen Christ had been silently and invisibly present when he, Thomas, had spoken them.

In an instant, Thomas realized that the resurrection of Jesus was a fact that couldn't be denied. He also realized the meaning of that resurrection. It proved that Jesus was both Lord and God (v. 28).

Thomas' experience has value for each of us. Every believer struggles to believe at one time or another. We are all, as Thomas was, secondhand believers. We are called to believe on the basis of witnesses. The fact that we struggle shouldn't drive us to despair. We aren't Christians because we have full or perfect faith but rather because we have faith. Even weak faith is true faith.

When we find it hard to believe, we need to learn to doubt our doubts and believe our beliefs. We need to let Thomas remind us that there is sufficient evidence on which to base our faith. And we need to remember that we don't believe in Christ because He has answered every question that has ever popped into our minds but rather because He has given us answers that we can't get around.

-28-

From God's Word, the Bible...

If I had said, "I will speak thus,"
Behold, I would have been untrue to the generation of
Your children.
When I thought how to understand this,
It was too painful for me—
Until I went into the sanctuary of God;
Then I understood their end.

Psalm 73:15-17

"Help, I Think God Isn't Fair!"

Do you sometimes think God hasn't been fair to you? Have you stumbled over that problem? You have tried to live for the Lord, and troubles and hardships seem to dog your steps. Meanwhile, you look around and see people who don't have the slightest interest in God, and they are getting along very well.

Asaph, the author of Psalm 73, ran smack dab into this problem. He was trying to honor God, and what did he have to show for it? Let him answer:

> ...*all day long I have been plagued,*
> *And chastened every morning* (v. 14).

What a testimony! Asaph says he had difficulty all day and every day! Meanwhile, the wicked seemed to be living carefree lives (v. 5).

Asaph began looking at people who had no interest in

God, and it appeared to him as if they were getting along splendidly. Then he began looking at himself. He was trying to honor God with his life and obey His commandments. But he didn't seem to be doing so well.

What did Asaph notice about those ungodly people? He writes:

> *They are not in trouble as other men;*
> *Nor are they plagued like other men* (v. 5).

For a moment Asaph let himself imagine that those wicked people living such easy lives must surely die hard. But as he thought about that, he realized it was not the case. He says:

> *There are no pangs in their death,*
> *But their strength is firm* (v. 4).

So far as Asaph could tell, the wicked pretty much had it made—they were living easy lives and dying easy deaths. On top of that was their attitude. One would expect such people to show a smidgen of gratitude and a dash of humility, but these people seemed to go about without either. They were brandishing pride as though it were a chain around their necks (v. 6). They didn't hesitate to speak "loftily" (v. 8). Instead of thanking God for the things they were enjoying, they "set their mouth against the heavens" (v. 9).

Asaph couldn't help but wonder. Shouldn't living for God count for something? It wasn't so much that he was wishing that the wicked would do worse than he. It was rather that he was wishing that he could do as well as they.

Prosperity for the wicked and adversity for the righteous—it wasn't fair! It seemed to Asaph as if God wasn't paying attention (v. 11) because it was obvious to him,

Asaph, that God would certainly set matters right if only He were aware of them.

Life in this world is never a sufficient basis for determining who is doing well and who is not doing well. Asaph needed the long view, and that is exactly what he got when he went to the house of God. How thankful we should be for God's house where we are rescued from the short view of things and given the long view!

There in God's house Asaph saw how foolish it is to envy people who don't know God. They may appear to be doing all right, but they are standing on slippery ground (v. 18). Each day could be their last day, and each breath their last breath, and then eternity!

When I find myself walking in Asaph's footprints, it is very helpful for me to remember that the unbeliever on his best day is far worse off than the believer on his worst day.

Asaph came out in a good place. He realized that no matter how bad his circumstances were, he had God. God was with him in every situation of life, and God is the greatest of all treasures. So we find him saying:

> *Nevertheless I am continually with You;*
> *You hold me by my right hand,*
> *You will guide me with Your counsel,*
> *And afterward receive me to glory.*
> (vv. 23-24)

When the devil suggests to those of us who know the Lord that He is being unfair to us, let's learn from Asaph to take the long view. And let's learn to ask ourselves this question: How it is possible for the One who through His Son is giving us eternal life in heaven to ever be unfair to us? If He never blessed us with anything else, we would still be immeasurably blessed.

-29-

From God's Word, the Bible...

But Zion said, "The LORD has forsaken me,
And my Lord has forgotten me."
"Can a woman forget her nursing child,
And not have compassion on the son of her womb?
Surely they may forget,
Yet I will not forget you.
See, I have inscribed you on the palms of My hands;
Your walls are continually before Me.

Isaiah 49:14-16

"Help, I Think God Has Forgotten Me!"

The last twenty-seven chapters of Isaiah are a marvel. The prophet was enabled by the Spirit of God to look down the corridor of time and see his people in captivity in Babylon. And the Spirit prompted Isaiah to write these chapters to provide comfort for those captives. The prophet was enabled to see so that he might soothe.

We can't begin to grasp all of the sorrows that the captivity brought to those people. Right at the top of the list of those sorrows was the feeling that God had abandoned them (v. 14).

As we read their melancholy words, we might be saying of ourselves: "Been there. Done that." It's common for God's people to go through such heart-wrenching problems that they think God has forsaken them and forgotten them.

But that is never the case. It may seem to be true, but it isn't true. Through Isaiah, the Lord let those people know that He hadn't forgotten them. He conveys His ongoing concern and care for them by using three figures. The first is *the devoted mother* (v. 15).

We can all think of instances in which mothers have indeed abandoned their children, but those instances are unusual and exceptional. When we hear the word "mother," the thing that immediately comes to mind is faithfulness and not faithlessness.

God assures His people that He is not like the rare mother who does forsake her children. What is generally true of mothers—refusing to forsake their children—is most certainly true of Him. He emphatically says: "I will not forget you."

The Lord proceeds to add *the figure of the inscribed hands* (v. 16a).

People in those days would often write the name of their god on their hands. Here God tells the captives that He had written their names on the palms of His hands. Written? No! It's much stronger than that. Writing can be erased. God had *inscribed* or engraved their names on His hands.

It's impossible for us to forget words that are indelibly etched on the psalms of our hands. Those words are ever before us, and God's people are ever before Him. Even when it seems that He has forgotten them? Yes, even when it seems that He has forgotten them! The God who has written us on His hands can never "write us off."

The final picture the Lord uses to assure His people is that of *the still standing walls* (v. 16b).

If someone had mentioned the walls of Jerusalem to those captives, they would have been quick to speak along these lines: "The walls of Jerusalem don't exist. The Babylonians knocked them down. And those destroyed walls prove that God doesn't care about us anymore."

But God said those destroyed walls were "continually" before Him. Here is a blessed thing! Where those captives saw ruins, God saw walls. This was His way of assuring them that the captivity was not the final word for them. He would in due time bring them out of captivity, restore them to the land of Judah, and the walls of Jerusalem would stand again. God's word of judgment is never His final word for His people.

The devil still points to our harsh circumstances (some of which, like the captives of old, we have brought upon ourselves) as proofs that God has forgotten us. We should respond by pointing him to those captives in Babylon and what God said to them. But we do even better if we point him to the cross of Christ. That is the supreme proof that God loves His people even more than a devoted mother loves her child.

As we gaze at that cross, we must surely see the proof that God has engraved the names of His people on His hands. God would never have allowed the hands of His Son to be nailed to that cross if He didn't have our names on His hands.

And God did it all so that He might replace the ruins of our sin with the walls of His salvation.

We can be confident that God will never forsake His people. But there was a time when He did forsake someone. That time was on the cross. There He actually forsook His Son so all who believe in Christ will never be God-forsaken in eternity (Matt. 27:46). Have you believed on Him?

-30-

From God's Word, the Bible...

*Buy the truth, and do not sell it,
Also wisdom and instruction and understanding.*

Proverbs 23:23

Purchasing and Preserving

This verse calls us to both make a purchase and to preserve what we purchase. We are to buy the truth and not sell it.

To make this purchase, we must first believe that there is such a thing as truth. We can't purchase something that doesn't exist. Many tell us that there is no such thing as absolute truth. They state as an absolute truth that there is no such thing as absolute truth! What an incredible irony!

I answer them with an absolute truth of my own—they are wrong, dead wrong!

There is such a thing as truth, and there is one truth that is more important than any other: it is the truth of the Bible. On the night before He was crucified, the Lord Jesus said to God the Father: "Your word is truth" (John 17:17; see also Ps. 119:142,151). Jesus, the God-man from heaven, would be the one to know.

The Bible does not contain all that is true, but all that is in the Bible is true! How blessed we are to have it!

We are to purchase the truth of the Bible. We can purchase a Bible without purchasing the truth of it. To purchase something is to pay the price for it. What is the price of the truth of the Bible? It is diligent study! We have not purchased the truth if we merely know the Bible is the Word of God. We must burrow into it by reading it, studying it, and listening to it proclaimed, remembering as we do these lines from Joseph Hart:

> *These hath God married, and no man shall part:*
> *Dust on the Bible and drought in the heart.*

If we're not studying the Bible as we should, it is accumulating dust; and no good comes from a dusty Bible. Dust on the Bible equals, Hart says, drought in the heart. We might say dust on the Bible creates dust in the heart. What kind of dust? Spiritual dust! The dust that robs us of spiritual vitality and productivity!

All that is in the Bible is true and all of its truth is important, but there is one truth in the Bible that is more important than all the others. That is the truth about the Lord Jesus Christ. As a matter of fact, He is the central theme of the Bible (Luke 24:27,44). Take Him out and you have no Bible left!

The Bible reveals both the truth of Jesus' person (who He was) and His work (what He did to provide salvation for sinners).

Who was He? God! What did He do? He added to His deity our humanity. So He was now fully God and fully man—the God-man! In our humanity, He lived in perfect obedience to God. Then He died on the cross to receive the wrath of God in the place of sinners. After that He arose from the grave and ascended to the Father in heaven. This is the gospel! This is the truth! And what precious truth it is! It is soul-saving truth for the sinner and soul-thrilling truth for the saint.

We must buy this truth. What is its price? Is it a thousand dollars? A million? Ten million? If eternal life could actually be purchased with dollars, many people would be willing to spend a great sum for it. But the purchase price isn't a matter of dollars. Salvation through Christ is free. To buy the truth about Christ simply means we must hear it and heed it.

The Bible says receiving Christ is a matter of believing in Him (John 3:16,36; Acts 16:31). Have we really heard this? Have we really heeded it?

After purchasing the truth, especially the truth of the gospel, we are to preserve it. That means we are to hold on to it at all costs. We are not to "sell out" to false teachers and their teachings, no matter how popular and appealing they may be.

When it comes to the truth, far too many of us are sellers rather than buyers! It's a brutal fact that many will fall for Bible-denying, Christ-denying teachings if those teachings are presented in a humorous and entertaining way. Let us not be counted in their number. Let us know the truth of the Bible, love that truth, and never sell out.

-31-

From God's Word, the Bible...

And He said to me, "My grace is sufficient for you, for My strength is made perfect in weakness."
Therefore most gladly I will rather boast in my infirmities, that the power of Christ may rest upon me.

2 Corinthians 12:9

Wisdom from Annie Johnson Flint

Annie Johnson Flint (1866-1932) encountered much hardship in life. When she was only three, her mother died. Her father, stricken with serious disease, arranged for the Flint family to take custody of his children.

Annie had just begun her career of teaching when she was afflicted with arthritis. The disease worsened until it made her an invalid. Her foster parents also died only months apart, leaving Annie and her sister alone and facing financial hardship. These circumstances were such that they would seem to have knocked the faith right out of Annie. But they didn't. Annie had come to faith in Christ when she was only eight years of age, and that faith grew stronger as she traveled her difficult and challenging path. Her problems prompted her to write hymns in which she expressed confidence in God's loving grace and sufficient grace. These may very well be the best-known lines that she ever wrote:

He giveth more grace when the burdens grow greater;
He sendeth more strength when the labors increase.
To added affliction He addeth His mercy;
To multiplied trials, His multiplied peace.
His love has no limit; His grace has no measure.
His power has no boundary known unto men.
For out of His infinite riches in Jesus,
He giveth, and giveth, and giveth again.

The trials I have experienced in life haven't come near those that Annie Johnson Flint knew, but I have often sung my difficulties away with those wonderful words. I have also been immensely blessed by these lines from Annie:

God hath not promised skies always blue,
Flower-strewn pathways all our lives through;
God hath not promised sun without rain,
Joy without sorrow, peace without pain.

God hath not promised we shall not know
Toil and temptation, trouble and woe;
He hath not told us we shall not bear
Many a burden, many a care.

God hath not promised smooth roads and wide,
Swift, easy travel, needing no guide;
Never a mountain, rocky and steep,
Never a river, turbid and deep.

But God hath promised strength for the day,
Rest for the labor, light for the way,
Grace for the trials, help from above,
Unfailing sympathy, undying love.

We needlessly add to the weight of our burdens when we take them to mean that God has failed to keep His promises to us. It's the devil who wants us to think that God has promised to do things for us that He has not promised. And he keeps us from laying claim to what God has promised.

Annie Johnson Flint had a clear view of what God hasn't promised and what He has. God has never promised that our skies will always be cloudless and blue. He has never promised flower-strewn paths, sun without rain, smooth roads and easy travel. If we think that He has promised these things, we will be bitter toward Him when difficulties come our way, and that will keep us from drawing comfort from the things He has promised—strength for the day, rest for the labor, light for the way, grace for the trials, and help from above.

And the best of all that God has promised us is His unfailing sympathy and undying love. If we doubt that sympathy and love, we must look to the cross until this logic is drilled into our hearts: If God would go to that extent to save us, He will never fail to love us. And, hard as it is for us to believe, our trials are part of that love.

Chris Machen calls us to trust the Lord in these words:

Bow the knee;
Trust the heart of your Father when the answer
Goes beyond what you can see.
Bow the knee;
Lift your eyes toward heaven and believe the
One who holds eternity.
And when you don't understand the purpose of His plan,
In the presence of the King,
Bow the knee

I think that Annie must smile approvingly from heaven's glory when she hears the singing of those words.

About the Author

Roger Ellsworth is a retired pastor, active in ministry and writing, who lives in Jackson, Tennessee. He and his wife, Sylvia, love the message of the Bible, and they enjoy sharing the wonderful counsel of the Word of God in language that ordinary people can understand and appreciate.

Roger has written numerous books on the Christian faith, and has exercised a preaching ministry for over fifty years. His sermons are available to listen for free on SermonAudio.com.

The Series

Enjoy collecting the My Coffee Cup Meditations Series.

A Dog and A Clock 978-0-9988812-9-4 (Series#1)
The "Thumbs-Up" Man 978-0-9988812-5-6 (Series#2)
When God Blocks Our Path 978-0-9988812-4-9 (Series#3)
Fading Lines, Unfading Hope 978-0-9996559-1-7 (Series#4)
The Day the Milk Spilled 978-0-9965168-6-0 (Series#5)
"Where Are the Donuts?" 978-0-9965168-7-7 (Series#6)
Sure Signs of Heavenly Hope 978-0-9988812-1-8 (Series#7)
My Dog Knows It's Sunday 978-0-9996559-6-2 (Series#8)
Rover and the Cows 978-0-9996559-7-9 (Series#9)
Apples of Gold in Settings of Silver (Series#10)
Old Houses, New Houses (Series#11)
The Gold Key on the Silver Thread (Series#12)

Collect All the Books!

www.mycoffeecupmeditations.com

www.ingramcontent.com/pod-product-compliance
Lightning Source LLC
Chambersburg PA
CBHW070613010526
44118CB00012B/1502